The
smart cook

90 budget friendly recipes for the *ProPoints*® plan

SIMON &
SCHUSTER
ILLUSTRATED

London · New York · Sydney · Toronto · New Delhi

A CBS COMPANY

First published in Great Britain by Simon & Schuster UK Ltd, 2012
A CBS COMPANY

13 5 7 9 10 8 6 4 2

Simon & Schuster UK Ltd, 1st Floor, 222 Gray's Inn Road, London WC1X 8HB
www.simonandschuster.co.uk
Simon & Schuster Australia, Sydney
Simon & Schuster India, New Delhi

A CIP catalogue copy for this book is available from the British Library.

Weight Watchers Publications Team: Jane Griffiths, Nina McKerlie, Imogen Prescott and Donna Watts
Simon & Schuster Project Management: WordWorks *Photography:* Steve Baxter *Prop styling:* Rachel Jukes
Food styling: Moyra Fraser *Text design concept:* Fiona Andreanelli *Design and typesetting:* Isobel Gillan
Cover design: Smith & Gilmour

Colour reproduction by Dot Gradations Ltd, UK
Printed and bound in Singapore

Pictured on the front cover: Beef and Vegetable Stew, page 86
Pictured on the back cover: Lamb and Chick Pea Burgers, page 82; Chicken, Squash and Spinach Filo Pie, page 72;
Pappardelle Noodle Pot, page 64; Chocolate Sponge, page 100

The
smart cook

90 budget friendly recipes for the **ProPoints**® plan

Moyra Fraser and Emma Marsden

ProPoints® value logo: You'll find this easy to read **ProPoints** value logo on every recipe in this book. The logo represents the number of **ProPoints** values per serving each recipe contains. It is not an indication of the fillingness of a recipe.

Watchers Watchers **ProPoints** Weight Loss System is a simple way to lose weight. As part of the Weight Watchers **ProPoints** plan, you'll enjoy eating delicious, healthy, filling foods that help to keep you feeling satisfied for longer and in control of your portions.

Filling & Healthy foods are highlighted in green. Focus on these foods where you can – they are healthy choices that will help you to feel satisfied for longer.

V This symbol denotes a vegetarian recipe and assumes that, where relevant, free range eggs, vegetarian cheese, vegetarian virtually fat free fromage frais, vegetarian low fat crème fraîche and vegetarian low fat yogurts are used. Virtually fat free fromage frais, low fat crème fraîche and low fat yogurts may contain traces of gelatine so they are not always vegetarian. Please check the labels.

✳ This symbol denotes a dish that can be frozen. Unless otherwise stated, you can freeze the finished dish for up to 3 months. Defrost thoroughly and reheat until the dish is piping hot throughout.

Recipe notes

Egg size: Medium unless otherwise stated.

Raw eggs: Only the freshest eggs should be used. Pregnant women, the elderly and children should avoid recipes with eggs which are raw or not fully cooked.

All fruits and vegetables: Medium unless otherwise stated.

Chocolate: Use chocolate with a minimum of 70% cocoa solids.

Low fat spread: Where a recipe states to use a low fat spread, a light spread with a fat content of no less than 38% should be used.

Stock: Stock cubes should be used in the recipes, unless otherwise stated. Prepare them according to the packet instructions, unless directed otherwise.

Microwaves: Microwave timings are for an 850 watt microwave oven.

Low fat soft cheese: Where a recipe states to use low fat soft cheese, a soft cheese with a fat content of 5% or less should be used.

Recipe timings: These are approximate and only meant to be guidelines. Please note that the preparation time includes all the steps up to and following the main cooking time(s).

contents

Welcome to The Smart Cook, the cookbook that works alongside the *ProPoints* plan at the same time as helping you save money on your weekly shop. This book will give you lots of hints and tips to make the most of the food you buy and so maximise its potential. With 90 inspirational recipe ideas, many including Filling & Healthy foods and all written for the *ProPoints* plan, it will help you to stay on track while enjoying really tasty dishes.

What are Filling & Healthy Foods?

At the heart of the *ProPoints* plan are Filling & Healthy foods. These have been selected from each of the food groups and are the very best choices for satisfaction and health.

- Filling & Healthy foods are filling – they are low in energy density (in other words, they are bulky foods that are low in *ProPoints* values) and will help to keep you satisfied as you lose weight.
- Filling & Healthy foods are healthier – they are foods that have been carefully selected for their higher fibre content and/or lower salt, sugar and saturated fat content.
- Filling & Healthy foods are great value – whether they're zero *ProPoints* value fruit and veg, a medium salmon fillet for a *ProPoints* value of 6 or a 5 *ProPoints* value (150 g/5½ oz, cooked) portion of wholemeal pasta, you can be sure you'll get the best deal out of every *ProPoints* value that you spend.

You can find Filling & Healthy foods at a glance. They are shown throughout the cookbook highlighted in green, like this.

How do we develop the recipes?

The cookbook team at Weight Watchers work with some very talented cookery authors to develop the recipes, with the main focus being on taste and satisfaction. We ensure that everyone we work with has all the up to date information on the *ProPoints* plan so that our members can make the most of their *ProPoints* budget when deciding what to cook. Once the recipes are developed, we go along to see them photographed to make sure that what you see in this book is what you get at home and we taste the recipes too.

A little bit about the *ProPoints* plan

The *ProPoints* plan is based on the latest nutritional science and is Weight Watchers most flexible and liveable plan ever. Completely unique to Weight Watchers, it has been designed to work around your real life so you can control your weight whatever situation you find yourself in each day. The recipes will help you stay on track by providing you with the *ProPoints* values per recipe, and highlighting foods that are Filling & Healthy.

Hints & Tips

- **Cook from scratch** Cooking meals from scratch and from basic ingredients will make a big difference to your weekly spend. It gives you more control over your budget and you can opt for cheaper and healthier ingredients.

- **Plan ahead** Decide what your family is going to eat for the week ahead, then use the recipes to write your shopping list.

- **Store your veg** Keep vegetables in the fridge to last longer.

- **Meat-free** Meat-free meals tend to be cheaper, but with a good recipe they can be just as tasty.

- **Seasonal food** Be a clever shopper and buy in season. Seasonal food costs less as it is more likely to be home-grown by local producers. Seasonal food also tastes better and involves fewer air-miles, so it's better for the environment.

- **Buy loose** Loose fruit and vegetables can save you a few precious pounds over time, as you're likely to get just the amount you need.

- **Shop later** Supermarkets often decrease their prices to half or more of the original cost later in the day. Take a trip to the supermarket near you towards the end of the day if possible and you're guaranteed to find some bargains.

- **Shop local** If you have a local market, fruit and vegetables are often reduced towards the end of the day.

- **Shop online** By using online shopping facilities, you will tend to stick to your shopping list and will be less tempted by foods you don't really need.

- **Freeze it** Use your freezer to make the most of any supermarket special offers and cut costs.

- **Herbs** Dried herbs are very convenient to use and can be substituted for fresh herbs if you wish, although the flavour will be different. They have a more concentrated flavour than fresh herbs – roughly 1 teaspoon of dried herbs is equivalent to 1 tablespoon of chopped fresh herbs, with the exception of the stronger flavoured tarragon and rosemary where ½ a teaspoon is sufficient. Add dried herbs at the beginning of a recipe so the flavour has time to develop. Never use dried herbs as a garnish – only fresh herbs.

Soups & Salads

Bonfire Soup

Bring a splash of vibrant colour to the table with this creamy pumpkin soup. It's rich and satisfying.

Serves 6
5 *ProPoints* values per serving
30 *ProPoints* values per recipe
40 minutes preparation,
    25 minutes cooking
V ✳

1.5 kg (3 lb 5 oz) **pumpkin** or **butternut squash**, *peeled, de-seeded and chopped*
750 g (1 lb 10 oz) **sweet potato**, *peeled and chopped*
4 cm (1½ inches) **fresh root ginger**, *peeled and sliced thinly*
3 **leeks**, *chopped*
calorie controlled cooking spray
2.5 litres (4½ pints) vegetable stock
finely grated zest of an orange and the juice of 2 oranges
salt and freshly ground black pepper

For the seed pesto
50 g (1¾ oz) pumpkin seeds, toasted (see Cook's tip)
a large handful of **fresh parsley**
2 **garlic cloves**

1 Put the pumpkin and sweet potato pieces, ginger and chopped leek in a large, lidded, non stick saucepan. Spray the vegetables with the cooking spray and stir until coated.
2 Fry the vegetables over a medium heat, stirring all the time, until they begin to tinge with colour. Add a splash of water if they start to stick.
3 Pour in the vegetable stock, a large pinch of orange zest and the juice of 1½ oranges. Bring to the boil, reduce the heat, then cover and simmer for 20–25 minutes or until very tender.
4 Leave the soup to cool in the saucepan for 10 minutes then purée in a blender or with a hand blender.
5 To make the seed pesto, finely chop the pumpkin seeds, parsley and garlic together. Put in a small bowl and beat in the remaining orange juice and zest. Season well.
6 Reheat the soup, season, and serve with a spoonful of seed pesto to stir in.

Cook's tips The pumpkin soup will freeze without the pesto for up to 3 months. Thaw overnight, bring to the boil and simmer to reheat.

To use fresh pumpkin seeds, wash them in a colander under hot water until thoroughly cleaned. Spread out on absorbent kitchen paper and leave to dry overnight. Line a grill pan with foil and grill the dried seeds until golden brown or dry-fry in a large frying pan until golden. To use store-bought seeds, store them in an airtight container for up to 6 months and then toast for a few minutes in a dry frying pan when you need them.

Try this Other ways to use the seed pesto include stirring it through 60 g (2 oz) dried **brown basmati rice**, cooked according to packet instructions, before serving for an extra 6 ***ProPoints*** values per serving.

Use 750 g (1 lb 10 oz) **carrots** instead of pumpkin or butternut squash for the same ***ProPoints*** values per serving.

Double Bean and Ham Bowl

This filling soup is ideal for cooking a day ahead and will benefit from a night in the fridge to allow the flavours time to develop.

Serves 4
4 *ProPoints* values per serving
17 *ProPoints* values per recipe
25 minutes preparation, 45 minutes cooking

calorie controlled cooking spray
2 onions, diced
2 celery sticks, diced
1 large carrot, peeled and diced
1 small courgette or leek, diced
1 garlic clove, crushed
290 g can borlotti beans in water, drained and rinsed
400 g can butter beans in water, drained and rinsed
400 g can chopped tomatoes
50 g (1¾ oz) wholewheat conchigliette pasta (small shells)
50 g (1¾ oz) Savoy cabbage, shredded finely
125 g (4½ oz) wafer thin smoked ham, diced finely
a small handful of finely shredded fresh basil leaves

1 Heat a large non stick saucepan then spray with the cooking spray. Add all the diced vegetables with the garlic and cook, stirring, for 6 minutes until softened and beginning to colour.
2 Stir in all the beans with the tomatoes, pasta and cabbage. Using the empty tomato can, add four cans of cold water. Bring to the boil then reduce the heat to simmer for about 45 minutes until the vegetables are tender.
3 Stir in the diced ham and basil and serve, or cool, cover and chill overnight in the fridge.

Try this Use a 410 g can of mixed pulses in water, drained and rinsed, to replace the butter beans, for the same ***ProPoints*** values per serving.

Summer Greens Soup

A delightfully bright summery soup. Make the most of cheap greens when in season or use frozen vegetables – either way this soup is very economical. Serve with a 50 g (1¾ oz) wholemeal bread roll for an extra 3 ***ProPoints*** values per serving.

Serves 4
2 *ProPoints* values per serving
10 *ProPoints* values per recipe
25 minutes preparation, 15 minutes cooking
V

calorie controlled cooking spray
5 spring onions, chopped
300 g (10½ oz) fresh or frozen peas
275 g (9½ oz) lettuce, e.g. Romaine or Cos, chopped
1.5 litres (2¾ pints) vegetable stock
40 g (1½ oz) half fat crème fraîche
a handful of fresh mint leaves
salt and freshly ground black pepper

1 Heat a medium non stick saucepan until hot. Spray the base with the cooking spray then add the spring onions. Cook, stirring occasionally, over a medium heat for 2 minutes. Add the peas, lettuce and stock and stir briefly.
2 Bring to the boil, reduce the heat and simmer, uncovered, for 15 minutes until the vegetables are very soft. Set aside to cool for 4–5 minutes.
3 In a blender, or with a hand blender, purée the soup with the crème fraîche and half the mint leaves, until almost smooth. Add a little extra stock to thin if necessary, season, and serve sprinkled with the remaining mint.

Try this Spoon the crème fraîche on to the hot soup, rather than blending it in, then garnish with the mint leaves and some extra ground black pepper.

Swap the peas for the same weight of broccoli florets for 1 ***ProPoints*** value per serving.

Spiced Cauliflower and Cumin Soup

Creamy cauliflower and toasted cumin seeds blend together to make a gently spiced soup that costs very little and takes minutes to make.

Serves 4
3 ProPoints values per serving
11 ProPoints values per recipe
35 minutes in total
V

½ teaspoon cumin seeds
calorie controlled cooking spray
2 onions, chopped
4 spring onions, chopped
½ teaspoon ground turmeric (optional)
500 g (1 lb 2 oz) cauliflower florets, chopped
350 g (12 oz) potatoes, peeled and diced
1.5 litres (2¾ pints) vegetable stock
150 g pot 0% fat Greek yogurt
2 tablespoons finely chopped fresh coriander or parsley
salt and freshly ground black pepper

1 Heat a medium, lidded, non stick saucepan and add the cumin. Stir over a medium heat for 1 minute until lightly toasted. Spray with the cooking spray and stir in the onions and the spring onions. Cover and cook for 4–5 minutes, stirring occasionally. Add a splash of water if the onions start to stick.
2 Add the turmeric (if using), cauliflower, potato and stock, stir briefly, and bring to the boil. Reduce the heat, cover, and simmer for 10 minutes until the cauliflower and potato are very tender.
3 Leave the soup to cool for 10 minutes then stir in half the yogurt and half the chopped herb. Purée the soup in a blender or with a hand blender until smooth and speckled with green. Season and reheat gently before serving with a spoonful of the remaining yogurt and a sprinkling of the chopped herb.

Cook's tip The turmeric gives the soup a wonderful pale yellow colour and mild spicy flavour, but the soup is just as good without it if you don't have any in the storecupboard. Remember, soups made with potato are best cooked and enjoyed on the same day.

Try this Swap half the potato for the same weight of sweet potato for the same **ProPoints** values per serving.

Parsnip and Rosemary Soup

The cheesy toasted breadcrumbs freeze well, so make double and freeze half to sprinkle over soups and salads.

Serves 6
4 ProPoints values per serving
23 ProPoints values per recipe
50 minutes preparation, 20 minutes cooking
V ✳

900 g (2 lb) parsnips, peeled and diced
calorie controlled cooking spray
2 fresh rosemary stalks, plus extra to garnish
zest of a large orange, pared in strips
3 large onions, chopped finely
juice of 2 large oranges
2 litres (3½ pints) vegetable stock
6 tablespoons skimmed milk
salt and freshly ground black pepper

For the crispy cheesy crumbs
1 slice Weight Watchers malted Danish bread
15 g (½ oz) half fat Cheddar cheese, grated

1 Put the parsnips in a large lidded non stick saucepan. Spray with the cooking spray and stir together until lightly coated. Add the rosemary and two or three strips of the pared orange zest. Fry the parsnips, stirring all the time, for 3–5 minutes, until they begin to turn golden at the edges. Add the onion with a splash of water and continue to fry for a further 2–3 minutes until the onion begins to soften.
2 Remove the orange zest and pour in the orange juice and stock. Bring to the boil, reduce the heat, then cover and simmer for 15–20 minutes or until the parsnips and onions are very soft. Leave to cool for 10 minutes.
3 Meanwhile, to make the crispy cheesy crumbs, blend or chop the bread into rough crumbs. Spread on a non stick baking sheet and sprinkle over the cheese. Grill under a medium grill, stirring occasionally, until the crumbs are evenly browned and the cheese is melted, then leave to cool.
4 When the soup has cooled, remove the rosemary from the soup, add the milk and blend the soup in a blender or with a hand blender until smooth. Add a little extra stock if the texture is too thick. Season and reheat gently, then serve with the crispy cheesy crumbs and a sprinkling of fresh rosemary.

Smoky Haddock Chowder

A filling soup that takes just minutes to make. Small pieces of smoked fish can be bought for a few pence from the fish counter of any large supermarket.

Serves 4

5 ProPoints values per serving
21 ProPoints values per recipe
40 minutes preparation, 30 minutes cooking

calorie controlled cooking spray
250 g (9 oz) potatoes, *unpeeled and diced*
1 leek, *sliced*
2 onions, *diced*
2 celery *sticks, diced*
400 ml (14 fl oz) skimmed milk
400 ml (14 fl oz) fresh vegetable stock or water
2 bay leaves
150 g (5½ oz) frozen sweetcorn
225 g (8 oz) skinless smoked haddock
a squeeze of lemon juice
a small handful of finely chopped fresh parsley

1 Spray a large non stick saucepan with the cooking spray. Add the potato, leek, onion and celery and spray again with the cooking spray. Cook, stirring occasionally, over a medium heat for 3–4 minutes. Add a splash of water if the vegetables begin to stick.

2 Add half the milk, the stock and the bay leaves. Bring to the boil then reduce the heat and simmer for about 30 minutes until all the vegetables are tender. Leave to cool for 10 minutes. Remove the bay leaves, then whizz 3–4 ladles of the soup in a blender till roughly puréed and return to the saucepan. Alternatively, use a hand blender in the saucepan for 10–15 seconds.

3 Add the remaining milk, sweetcorn and the smoked fish to the soup and simmer gently for a further 5–7 minutes. Break up and flake the fish through the soup using a wooden spoon. Add a squeeze of lemon juice, scatter over the parsley, and serve.

Cook's tip The soup should need no other seasoning as the smoked fish adds sufficient natural salt.

Try this Swap the fish for the same weight of chopped smoked ham for 6 **ProPoints** values per serving.

Hot and Sour Mushroom Soup

The beauty of this recipe is that the taste improves with time, so this Asian inspired soup is ideal for making the day before.

Serves 4

1 ProPoints value per serving
2 ProPoints values per recipe
10 minutes preparation, 30 minutes cooking
V ✳

300 g (10½ oz) chestnut mushrooms, *sliced very thinly*
1 yellow or red pepper, *de-seeded and sliced thinly*
2 spring onions, *shredded thinly*
1.2 litres (2 pints) vegetable stock
¼ red chilli, *de-seeded and diced*
2 tablespoons white wine vinegar
4 tablespoons light soy sauce
a small handful of roughly chopped fresh coriander, *to garnish*
salt and freshly ground black pepper

1 Put the first five ingredients in a medium saucepan and bring to the boil. Reduce the heat and simmer, uncovered, for about 30 minutes.

2 Add the vinegar and soy sauce. Season, if necessary, and stir in the coriander just before serving.

Cook's tips If you want to control the level of heat, put the ¼ chilli in the soup whole and remove it before adding the vinegar in step 2.

Freeze the cooled soup without the coriander. Reheat until piping hot and stir in the coriander just before serving.

Moroccan Spice Pot

This richly flavoured soup, spiced with an aromatic North African paste, is the perfect meal-in-a-bowl soup for a cold day. Serve with 1 tablespoon 0% fat Greek yogurt per person for an additional 1 *ProPoints* value per serving.

Serves 4
3 *ProPoints* values per serving
11 *ProPoints* values per recipe
25 minutes preparation, 45 minutes cooking
V

calorie controlled cooking spray
100 g (3½ oz) potatoes, unpeeled and diced
100 g (3½ oz) leeks, chopped
100 g (3½ oz) carrots, peeled and chopped
1 small onion, chopped
150 g (5½ oz) fennel or celery, chopped
2 teaspoons harissa paste
1.2 litres (2 pints) vegetable stock
390 g can green lentils in water, drained and rinsed
100 g (3½ oz) spinach leaves
juice of ½ a lemon
salt and freshly ground black pepper

1 Spray a large non stick saucepan with the cooking spray. Add the potato, leek, carrot, onion and fennel or celery and spray again with the cooking spray. Cook, stirring occasionally, over a medium heat for 3–4 minutes. Add a splash of water if the vegetables begin to stick.
2 Stir in the harissa and stock. Bring to the boil, then reduce the heat and simmer for 45 minutes until all the vegetables are tender. With a hand blender, whizz the soup for 10–15 seconds to purée some of the mixture.
3 Stir in the lentils and simmer for a further 10 minutes. Add the spinach and cook, stirring, for 1–2 minutes until just wilted. Season and add a squeeze of lemon juice to taste before serving.

Cook's tip Harissa is a Moroccan spice paste, a blend of cumin, coriander, caraway and chilli and will last for up to 3 weeks in the fridge.

Spicy Pork Pho

This terrific spicy broth makes a lovely lunch or light supper.

Serves 4
5 *ProPoints* values per serving
21 *ProPoints* values per recipe
30 minutes preparation, 15 minutes cooking

a small handful of fresh coriander
1 garlic clove, crushed
200 g (7 oz) lean pork mince
25 g (1 oz) rolled porridge oats
calorie controlled cooking spray
1 small red chilli, halved and de-seeded
2.5 cm (1 inch) piece fresh root ginger, peeled and sliced
1 lemongrass stalk, split almost in two horizontally
150 g (5½ oz) sugar snap peas or mange tout
150 g (5½ oz) baby sweetcorn, sliced diagonally
150 g (5½ oz) ready-to-wok medium egg noodles
6 tablespoons light soy sauce
2 litres (3½ pints) fresh vegetable stock or water
4 spring onions, shredded
1 lime, quartered, to serve

1 Finely chop half of the coriander. Mash the chopped coriander and garlic into the pork with the oats, using a fork. Roll the mixture into 24 small, walnut-sized balls.
2 Spray a non stick frying pan with the cooking spray. Fry the pork balls over a high heat, a few at a time, until golden all over. Remove to a plate and set aside.
3 Put the chilli, ginger and lemongrass in a medium saucepan, add the pork balls and all the remaining ingredients, except the spring onions, the remaining coriander and the lime.
4 Bring to the boil, then reduce the heat and simmer for 15 minutes until the vegetables and pork balls are cooked. Roughly chop the remaining coriander and stir in with the spring onions. Serve with wedges of lime to squeeze over the soup.

Try this Turkey mince can be swapped for the pork for the same *ProPoints* values per serving.

Chicken Noodle Broth

This soup can be frozen so you've got an ideal lunch or light supper to hand for when you don't feel like cooking.

Serves 4

5 ProPoints values per serving

20 ProPoints values per recipe

30 minutes preparation,
   55 minutes cooking

*

calorie controlled cooking spray

2 large carrots, peeled and diced finely

3 celery sticks, diced finely

2 Spanish onions or 4 regular onions,
   diced finely

2 large garlic cloves, sliced thinly

a small handful of fresh thyme

1 bay leaf

1.5 litres (2¾ pints) vegetable stock

400 g (14 oz) skinless chicken drumsticks

75 g (2¾ oz) dried spaghetti

a small handful of finely chopped
   fresh parsley

1 Heat a lidded non stick saucepan, spray with the cooking spray and cook the carrots, celery, onion and garlic for 6 minutes, stirring, until beginning to colour. Add a splash of water if the vegetables begin to stick.

2 Stir in the thyme, bay leaf and stock then bring to the boil. Reduce the heat and carefully drop in the chicken. Simmer very gently, covered, for 45 minutes.

3 Remove the chicken to a plate and pull the flesh from the bones. Discard the bones.

4 Meanwhile, break the spaghetti into the hot soup and simmer, uncovered, for 10 minutes until tender.

5 Return all the chicken to the saucepan with the parsley and reheat gently before serving.

Cook's tip It's very easy to pull the chicken from the bones if you use two forks.

Try this If you like the flavour of ginger, swap the thyme, bay leaf and parsley for 2.5 cm (1 inch) sliced fresh root ginger and stir in a small handful of chopped fresh coriander just before serving.

Lemon and Artichoke Salad

This zesty rocket, toasted almond and artichoke salad is ideal for summer. Serve with a simple herb omelette made with 2 eggs per person for an extra 4 **ProPoints** values per serving.

Serves 4
4 ProPoints values per serving
14 ProPoints values per recipe
15 minutes in total
V

280 g jar artichoke hearts in oil, drained, oil reserved
100 g bag rocket
½ cucumber, sliced thinly
25 g (1 oz) toasted flaked almonds

For the lemon and thyme dressing
2 teaspoons wholegrain mustard
2 teaspoons honey
2 teaspoons lemon juice
2 teaspoons artichoke oil (from the jar)
a small handful of roughly chopped fresh thyme
salt and freshly ground black pepper

1 Make the dressing by whisking together all the ingredients with plenty of seasoning and set aside.
2 Arrange the artichokes on small serving plates and pile the rocket and cucumber on top. Sprinkle with the toasted almonds and dressing and serve immediately.

Cook's tip When fresh artichokes are in season, cook two in boiling water for 30–40 minutes or until one of the leaves can be pulled away easily. Drain the artichokes, cool and quarter. Remove all the hairy choke from the base of the artichoke and serve as above, using 2 teaspoons of olive oil to replace the oil from the jar. The **ProPoints** values will be 3 per serving.

Beetroot in a Bag

Considering its simplicity, this is surprisingly intense in flavour. Smaller summer beetroots are best for this dish as they have an almost smoky taste when roasted.

Serves 4
0 ProPoints values per serving
1 ProPoints value per recipe
10 minutes preparation, 1½ hours cooking
V

450 g (1 lb) raw beetroot, unpeeled and as small as you can find
2 garlic cloves, crushed
a small handful of fresh oregano, chopped roughly
2 tablespoons balsamic vinegar
juice of an orange
1 teaspoon light muscovado sugar
salt and freshly ground black pepper

1 Preheat the oven to Gas Mark 6/200°C/fan oven 180°C. Lay a large, double thickness of foil on the work surface and put the beetroot in the centre.
2 Put all the other ingredients in a small saucepan and warm together until the sugar dissolves. Season.
3 Bring the sides of the foil up and scrunch together to form a bag. Pour in the warm vinegar mixture and pinch the top of the foil to seal.
4 Bake in the oven for about 1½ hours or until very tender. Serve the beetroot with the warm cooking juices.

Cook's tip To test if the beetroot is cooked, open the bag and push the point of a skewer into the beetroot. It should slide in easily.

Ham and Pear Salad

Cured ham, pear and tangy mango combine to make a salad that's fresh and clean-tasting. Simple and quick to make for a light lunch or a starter for supper.

Serves 2

4 *ProPoints* values per serving
8 *ProPoints* values per recipe
15 minutes in total

4 slices prosciutto ham
2 pears, cored and sliced thinly
50 g (1¾ oz) salad leaves
1 small courgette, pared into thin strips

For the mango and orange dressing
1 tablespoon smooth mango chutney
4 tablespoons fresh orange juice,
*   squeezed or bought*
1 teaspoon olive oil
1–2 teaspoons lemon juice, to taste
salt and freshly ground black pepper

For the garlic crumbs
1 slice Weight Watchers Danish malted
*   brown bread*
1 garlic clove, halved

1 To make the garlic crumbs, rub the bread all over with the cut side of the garlic and toast in a toaster or under the grill until golden on both sides. Leave to cool then crumble or chop into rough crumbs and season.

2 Whisk together all the dressing ingredients and season.

3 When ready to serve, divide the ham between two serving plates. Put the pear slices in a bowl and toss with the salad leaves, courgette and a little of the dressing. Divide the salad between the plates, sprinkle with the garlic crumbs, drizzle with the remaining dressing and serve immediately.

Cook's tips Look out for pretty 'rosy' pears and leave their skin on to enjoy the soft pink colour.

Market stalls often sell off ripe pears cheaply at the end of the day, so watch out for a bargain.

Try this Swap the pear for a small, ripe mango, peeled, stoned and sliced, for the same ***ProPoints*** values.

This fantastic salad makes the most of the classic and delicious combination of ham and fruit.

Red Lentil Salad with Greek Dressing

This salad is simple, cheap and quick with a surprising combination of textures. It's delicious with 110 g (4 oz) grilled fresh mackerel for an extra 6 *ProPoints* values per serving.

Serves 4
3 *ProPoints* values per serving
14 *ProPoints* values per recipe
15 minutes preparation, 15 minutes cooking
V

50 g (1¾ oz) dried red lentils, rinsed
200 g can sweetcorn in water, drained
2 peppers, de-seeded and diced

For the Greek dressing
a small handful of finely chopped fresh mint leaves
75 g (2¾ oz) 0% fat Greek yogurt
50 g (1¾ oz) cucumber, grated coarsely
1 teaspoon olive oil
1 tablespoon skimmed milk
a squeeze of lemon juice
salt and freshly ground black pepper

1 Put the lentils in a saucepan and cover with cold water. Bring to the boil then reduce the heat and simmer gently for about 15 minutes or until the lentils are just tender. Drain well and leave to cool.
2 Meanwhile, to make the dressing, stir the mint into the yogurt with the cucumber, olive oil and milk. Add a squeeze of lemon juice and some seasoning and set aside.
3 Mix together the lentils, sweetcorn and peppers. Spoon over a little of the dressing before serving. Hand the remaining dressing round separately.

Cook's tips Choose red or orange peppers for colour and texture, whichever are cheaper.

The dressing also makes an excellent sauce for grilled mackerel or lamb steaks.

Try this Swap the sweetcorn for 100 g (3½ oz) de-seeded, diced and steamed butternut squash for 2 *ProPoints* values per serving.

Spiced Turkey and Couscous Salad

This salad is bursting with flavour. With a fruity yogurt dressing, it's perfect for picnics.

Serves 4
8 *ProPoints* values per serving
30 *ProPoints* values per recipe
15 minutes in total + 5 minutes soaking

175 g (6 oz) dried wholewheat couscous
40 g (1½ oz) dried cranberries
a kettleful of boiling water
½ stock cube, crumbled
½ teaspoon ground turmeric
1 red onion, sliced from tip to root
100 g (3½ oz) courgette, grated coarsely
200 g pack wafer thin roast turkey, shredded
a small handful of fresh coriander or mint, or a mixture of both
75 g (2¾ oz) baby spinach leaves
grated zest of ½ an orange and the juice of an orange
salt and freshly ground black pepper

For the orange and yogurt dressing
150 g (5½ oz) 0% fat Greek yogurt
juice of an orange
2 tablespoons chopped fresh coriander or mint or a mixture of both

1 Put the couscous and dried cranberries in a bowl, pour over enough boiling water to cover, crumble in the stock cube and add the turmeric. Cover with a plate. Leave for 5 minutes or until the stock is absorbed and the grains are tender. Using a fork, fluff up the couscous and set aside.
2 Meanwhile, mix together all the dressing ingredients and season using plenty of black pepper.
3 Add the remaining salad ingredients to the couscous and season. Spoon over the dressing before serving.

Cook's tip The salad and the couscous can be made the day before. Keep, covered, in the fridge. Serve at room temperature.

V Try this For a vegetarian alternative, swap the shredded turkey for 2 hard boiled eggs, chopped roughly, for 7 *ProPoints* values per serving.

Black Eyed Bean Salad

A filling, fresh-tasting salad that tastes even better the next day. Serve with 50 g (1¾ oz) crumbled reduced fat feta cheese and spoon into a small warm pitta bread for 6 **ProPoints** values per serving.

Serves 4

2 ProPoints values per serving

8 ProPoints values per recipe

10 minutes in total + 1 hour marinating

V

400 g can black eyed beans in water, drained and rinsed

1 red or white onion, diced finely

4 spring onions, diced finely

2 green peppers, de-seeded and diced finely

½ cucumber, diced finely

½ green or red chilli, de-seeded and chopped finely

150 g (5½ oz) cherry tomatoes, quartered

2 tablespoons lemon juice

2 small handfuls finely chopped fresh parsley

1 Mix together the beans, onions, spring onions, pepper, cucumber, chilli and tomatoes. Stir in the lemon juice and parsley. Cover and set aside for at least 1 hour before eating.

Cook's tips You can keep the salad covered in the fridge for up to 3 days. Allow 15–20 minutes at room temperature again before eating.

You could use regular tomatoes instead of cherry tomatoes, if they're cheaper. Cut them into rough dice.

Try this Swap the black eyed beans for a 400 g can of kidney beans in water, drained and rinsed, or a 400 g can of green lentils in water, drained and rinsed, for the same **ProPoints** values.

Meat-free & Sides

These marvellous meat-free ideas are not only satisfying and appealing, they're also a great way to stretch your budget.

Roasted Squash Wedges

Here's a creative side dish or starter. You can use any winter squash variety or pumpkin, depending on what's available and in season.

Serves 4
2 *ProPoints* values per serving
9 *ProPoints* values per recipe
10 minutes preparation,
  50 minutes cooking
V

calorie controlled cooking spray
1 kg (2 lb 4 oz) squash, such as acorn or
  butternut, or pumpkin, unpeeled,
  de-seeded and cut into wedges or chunks
80 g (3 oz) half fat Cheddar cheese, grated
  coarsely
20 g (¾ oz) sunflower seeds
salt and freshly ground black pepper

1 Preheat the oven to Gas Mark 6/200°C/fan oven 180°C. Spray a shallow non stick roasting tin with the cooking spray and add the squash pieces. Spray again with the cooking spray and season. Roast the squash for about 40 minutes until tender and golden brown.
2 Remove the tray from the oven and sprinkle with the cheese and sunflower seeds. Return to the oven for a further 10 minutes until golden brown. Serve immediately.

Cook's tip There is no need to peel the squash as the skin softens when cooked and is delicious to eat.

Try this Swap the half fat Cheddar cheese for the same weight of reduced fat feta cheese or light mozzarella cheese, crumbled over the vegetables, for the same ***ProPoints*** values per person.

Grilled Aubergines with Feta Dressing

Grilled aubergines with salty feta cheese make a delicious Greek-style side dish.

Serves 2
5 *ProPoints* values per serving
11 *ProPoints* values per recipe
35 minutes in total
V

2 small **aubergines**
300 ml (10 fl oz) vegetable stock
calorie controlled cooking spray

For the feta dressing
150 g (5½ oz) **0% fat Greek yogurt**
4 tablespoons extra light mayonnaise
4 **spring onions**, chopped finely
a small handful of **fresh oregano** or **basil**
75 g (2¾ oz) reduced fat Greek salad cheese

1 Preheat the grill to medium high. Thickly slice each aubergine crosswise into about 6 slices. Layer the aubergines over the base of a large, deep, non stick frying pan. Pour over the vegetable stock. Bring to the boil, then reduce the heat and simmer very gently for about 10 minutes until just tender.
2 Meanwhile, make the feta dressing by beating together all the ingredients. Set aside.
3 Line a grill pan with foil and spray with the cooking spray. Lay the aubergine slices over the pan and spray again with the cooking spray.
4 Grill the aubergine till golden and slightly charred in places. Turn and continue to cook on the other side. Serve the aubergine hot with the feta dressing.

Cook's tip The aubergine will take 3–4 minutes to brown under the grill. Leave the slices until charred in places for a delicious smoky flavour.

Honeyed Red Onion Marmalade

This red onion marmalade is perfect to make and keep in the fridge, ready to perk up simple grilled skinless boneless chicken breast or oily fish such as mackerel. 2 teaspoons will be 1 *ProPoints* value.

Makes 24 teaspoonfuls
1 *ProPoints* value per serving
12 *ProPoints* values per recipe
25 minutes preparation, 45 minutes cooking
V

calorie controlled cooking spray
4 large red **onions**, sliced thinly
a small handful of **fresh thyme** or **rosemary** leaves
600 ml (20 fl oz) red grape juice
1 tablespoon honey
3 tablespoons balsamic vinegar
salt and freshly ground black pepper

1 Heat a medium, lidded, non stick saucepan and spray with the cooking spray. Add all the onions and herb and spray again with the cooking spray. Cook, covered, stirring regularly over a medium heat, for a good 15–20 minutes or until the onions are very soft and beginning to turn golden. Add a splash of water if the onions begin to stick.
2 Stir in the grape juice, honey and 1 tablespoon of the vinegar. Bring to the boil then reduce the heat and simmer very gently, uncovered, for a further 40–45 minutes until most of the liquid has evaporated and the onions are dark and sticky.
3 Season the onions and stir in the remaining balsamic vinegar. Spoon the onions into a large clean jar with a vinegar-proof lid, such as a Kilner jar. Cool and store in the fridge for up to 3 weeks.

Cook's tip Pure pressed grape juice is available in both chilled and long-life cartons. Don't confuse it with grape juice from concentrate or grape-based drinks.

Try this Alternatively, spoon the marmalade into hot baked Portobello **mushrooms** or into hot baked **sweet potatoes** and crumble a little reduced fat feta cheese on top before serving, remembering to add the *ProPoints* values.

Carrot and Cumin Mash

A simple way to transform humble carrots into a fragrant accompaniment. Why not make a batch and freeze some?

Serves 4
0 *ProPoints* values per serving
1 *ProPoints* value per recipe
25 minutes in total
V ✳

600 g (1 lb 5 oz) carrots, peeled and sliced
a kettleful of boiling water
½ vegetable stock cube
¼ teaspoon cumin seeds
juice of ½ an orange
a small handful of fresh coriander or parsley leaves,
   chopped finely
salt and freshly ground black pepper

1 Put the carrots in a medium saucepan and pour over just enough boiling water to cover. Add the stock cube and return to the boil. Reduce the heat and simmer gently, uncovered, until the carrots are very soft and tender.
2 Drain the carrots and reserve or freeze the stock for soups and gravies.
3 Meanwhile, heat a small frying pan and dry-fry the cumin seeds for 10–20 seconds until lightly toasted. Tip the seeds on to a wooden board and crush lightly with a pestle and mortar, the end of a rolling pin or the base of the frying pan.
4 Mash the carrots with the crushed cumin seeds, the orange juice, the coriander or parsley, and some seasoning.

Try this For a creamier mash, beat 40 g (1½ oz) 0% fat Greek yogurt into the carrots for no extra *ProPoints* values per serving.

Thai Slaw

If you thought coleslaw was boring, think again – this Thai-inspired mix makes a delicious side dish to serve with any simple grills or bakes.

Serves 4
2 *ProPoints* values per serving
8 *ProPoints* values per recipe
15 minutes in total + cooling
V

25 g (1 oz) sesame seeds
350 g (12 oz) crisp white cabbage, shredded finely
200 g (7 oz) carrots, peeled and grated coarsely
a bunch of spring onions, shredded
a handful of finely chopped fresh mint
¼ red chilli, de-seeded and chopped finely

For the Thai dressing
4 teaspoons light soft brown sugar
8 tablespoons light soy sauce
zest of a lime and juice of 2 limes

1 First make the Thai dressing by stirring together all the ingredients. Set aside.
2 Sprinkle the sesame seeds over the base of a small frying pan and dry-fry for 20–30 seconds until golden brown. Leave to cool.
3 In a large bowl, mix together the cabbage and carrots with the spring onions, mint, chilli and toasted sesame seeds.
4 Stir in the dressing, cover and leave the salad in a cool place for about 30 minutes. Stir well before serving.

Cook's tips Be careful when toasting sesame seeds since they brown very quickly.

The salad will keep in the fridge for up to 3 days. It will gradually lose a bit of crunch but will still be delicious.

Try this For a more substantial lunch or supper dish, add 100 g (3½ oz) cooked peeled prawns per person for 4 *ProPoints* values per serving.

Oven-roasted Ratatouille

This is a flexible, summery recipe that can be eaten as an accompaniment to grilled meat, prawns or fish, or just as it is for a light lunch, with 50 g (1¾ oz) crusty brown bread, for an extra 3 *ProPoints* values per serving.

Serves 4
0 *ProPoints* values per serving
1 *ProPoints* values per recipe
15 minutes preparation, 1 hour cooking
V ✳

calorie controlled cooking spray
225 g (8 oz) red or white onions, chopped roughly
300 g (10½ oz) courgettes, chopped roughly
300 g (10½ oz) aubergines, chopped roughly
3 peppers, de-seeded and chopped roughly
3 garlic cloves, peeled
1 tablespoon tomato purée
1 tablespoon capers in brine (optional)
225 ml (8 fl oz) hot vegetable stock
a small handful of finely chopped fresh parsley
salt and freshly ground black pepper

1 Preheat the oven to Gas Mark 6/200°C/fan oven 180°C. Spray the base of a large non stick roasting tin with the cooking spray. Put all the vegetables plus the garlic cloves in the tin and spray again with the cooking spray. Season and toss the vegetables together to mix.
2 Roast the vegetables, stirring occasionally, for about 40 minutes until almost tender.
3 Stir in the tomato purée, capers and hot stock and put the vegetables back in the oven for a further 15–20 minutes until very tender. Stir in the parsley and serve the ratatouille warm or cold.

Cook's tip The ratatouille freezes well so make a big batch and put some in the freezer.

Try this Stir 1 tablespoon balsamic vinegar and a small handful of chopped fresh basil into the roasted vegetables at the end of cooking time.

Sweet 'n' Sour Shallots

A good-looking side dish that goes well with just about anything. Try these shallots with simple roasts or grilled meats. They're also good served cold with salad.

Serves 4
1 *ProPoints* value per serving
3 *ProPoints* values per recipe
20 minutes preparation, 40 minutes cooking
V

750 g (1 lb 10 oz) shallots, peeled
calorie controlled cooking spray
400 ml (14 fl oz) vegetable stock
2 teaspoons honey
4 tablespoons balsamic vinegar
a small handful of fresh thyme leaves (optional)
salt and freshly ground black pepper

1 Halve any large shallots. Heat a large non stick saucepan and spray with the cooking spray. Add the shallots and spray again with the cooking spray. Stir over a high heat for 4–5 minutes until they begin to turn golden brown.
2 Pour in the stock, honey and half the vinegar. Bring to the boil then reduce the heat and simmer, uncovered, for 35–40 minutes, stirring occasionally. Simmer until most of the liquid has evaporated and the shallots are very tender.
3 Stir in the remaining vinegar, thyme (if using) and some seasoning. Serve the shallots warm or cold.

Cook's tips Look out for the larger 'torpedo' shaped shallots which you'll find in all the supermarkets. They're much easier and faster to peel than the button ones.

When peeling shallots, just trim the root end – don't cut it off. That way the shallots will stay whole when cooked.

The shallots can be cooked the day before and reheated gently on the hob to serve.

Okra Indian Style

Braised okra is a lovely, aromatic side dish for a meat or fish main meal.

Serves 4
0 *ProPoints* values per serving
1 *ProPoints* value per recipe
35 minutes in total
V

calorie controlled cooking spray
2 large onions, chopped finely
2 teaspoons mild tikka paste
450 g (1 lb) okra, trimmed and sliced horizontally
4 large tomatoes, chopped
1 teaspoon mustard seeds
a small handful of fresh coriander leaves
salt and freshly ground black pepper

1 Heat a large, lidded, non stick frying pan over a medium heat. Spray with the cooking spray then add the onions. Cook for 6 minutes, stirring occasionally, until soft. Add a splash of water if the onions begin to stick.
2 Stir in the tikka paste and cook for 1 minute then add the okra, tomatoes and mustard seeds. Season. Mix well and keep stirring gently, for about 10 minutes, until the tomatoes are pulpy.
3 Lower the heat. Add 2 tablespoons of water, cover and simmer for another 4–5 minutes. Sprinkle with coriander leaves just before serving.

Cook's tip Okra releases a sticky substance when cooked, but keep stirring gently and this will disappear.

Chilli Lime Noodles

Packed with a punch, these noodles can be fried and on the table in less than 20 minutes.

Serves 4
5 *ProPoints* values per serving
19 *ProPoints* values per recipe
15 minutes in total
V

calorie controlled cooking spray
375 g packet straight-to-wok rice noodles
4 spring onions, chopped finely
75 g (2¾ oz) frozen peas
freshly ground black pepper

For the chilli lime dressing
4 tablespoons light soy sauce
juice of a lime
½ red chilli, de-seeded and chopped finely
1 teaspoon sesame oil
1 teaspoon light muscovado sugar
finely grated zest of ½ an orange and the juice of an orange

1 To make the dressing, whisk together the soy sauce, lime juice, chilli, sesame oil and sugar with half the orange zest and all the juice. Set aside.
2 Heat a non stick wok or large non stick frying pan and spray with the cooking spray. Stir in the noodles, spring onions and peas. Cook, stirring, for 4–5 minutes or until piping hot.
3 Pour the dressing over the noodles and stir over a high heat for 1–2 minutes. Serve immediately, seasoned with black pepper and sprinkled with the remaining zest.

Cook's tips The chilli lime dressing is also delicious spooned over steamed salmon fillets or poached skinless chicken breast fillets. Alternatively, use as a salad dressing tossed through chopped Chinese leaves, sliced cucumber and shredded spring onions.

Make up a large batch of the dressing and then keep it in a jar in the fridge for up to 2 weeks.

If you want to cook the noodles yourself from dry, use 175 g (6 oz) and cook according to packet instructions, for the same ***ProPoints*** values per serving.

Spring Greens Risotto

Enjoy this hearty vegetarian supper any night of the week. You can use sliced leek in winter instead of the courgette.

Serves 2
9 *ProPoints* values per serving
18 *ProPoints* values per recipe
45 minutes in total
V

275 ml (9½ fl oz) vegetable stock
calorie controlled cooking spray
1 small onion, chopped
1 garlic clove, crushed
150 g (5½ oz) courgette, diced
120 g (4½ oz) dried Arborio rice
50 g (1¾ oz) fresh or frozen peas
100 g (3½ oz) fresh or frozen broad beans
4 spring onions, chopped
20 g (¾ oz) Parmesan cheese, grated finely

1 Put the stock in a medium saucepan and bring to the boil then reduce to a gentle simmer.
2 Heat a medium size, non stick frying pan and spray with the cooking spray. Add the onion, garlic and courgette and spray again with the cooking spray. Cook for 3–4 minutes, stirring regularly.
3 Stir the rice into the pan, over a medium heat, and add the stock a ladleful at a time, stirring frequently between each addition. Simmer gently before adding more and continue until you have one ladleful left and the rice is almost tender.
4 Stir in the peas and broad beans with the last of the stock and simmer again until the stock has been absorbed, the rice is tender and the vegetables are just cooked.
5 Preheat the grill to high. Stir the spring onions into the risotto and sprinkle with the grated cheese. Put the pan under the grill for 2–3 minutes until the cheese is melted and golden. Serve immediately.

Cook's tip Make sure each ladleful of stock has been absorbed before adding another.

Try this With the last ladleful of stock add 125 g (4½ oz) raw salmon fillet. Simmer with the risotto for a few minutes until cooked, for 12 ***ProPoints*** values per serving.

Spiced Lentil and Egg Supper

A satisfying supper for all the family. All that's needed to accompany it is a large dish of steamed seasonal vegetables such as broccoli, peas or spring greens.

Serves 4
7 *ProPoints* values per serving
30 *ProPoints* values per recipe
40 minutes in total
V

150 g (5½ oz) dried brown basmati rice
50 g (1¾ oz) dried split red lentils, rinsed
1 vegetable stock cube, crumbled
1 teaspoon dried turmeric
calorie controlled cooking spray
1 large onion, chopped finely
1 aubergine
3 garlic cloves, crushed
100 g (3½ oz) button mushrooms, diced
150 g (5½ oz) frozen peas
a squeeze of lemon juice
4 eggs
salt and freshly ground black pepper

1 Put the rice and lentils in a medium saucepan and add the stock cube and half the turmeric with plenty of cold water. Bring to the boil then reduce the heat and simmer gently for 20–25 minutes, or until the rice is just tender.
2 Heat a medium non stick saucepan and spray with the cooking spray. Add the onion, aubergine and garlic and spray again with the cooking spray. Cook, stirring, for about 6 minutes until softened. Add a splash of water if the vegetables begin to stick. Stir in the remaining turmeric and the mushrooms and cook for a further 5–7 minutes, stirring all the time, until all the vegetables are soft.
3 Meanwhile, soft-boil the eggs. Bring a pan of water to a simmer and then add the eggs and let them cook for 5–7 minutes, depending on how soft you want them to be.
4 Add the frozen peas to the cooked vegetables and stir over a medium heat until heated through. Drain the rice and lentils and stir into the cooked vegetables. Check the seasoning and add a squeeze of lemon juice to taste. Serve the rice and lentils in bowls, each topped with a soft boiled egg.

Thai Omelette

This simple omelette filled with a generous handful of vegetables, tossed in a sweet and spicy dressing, is ideal for lunch.

Serves 1
4 *ProPoints* values per serving
4 *ProPoints* values per recipe
20 minutes in total
V

juice of a lime
1 teaspoon soy sauce
1 teaspoon sweet chilli sauce
1 small carrot, peeled and cut into matchsticks
50 g (1¾ oz) beansprouts
75 g (2¾ oz) Chinese cabbage, shredded
¼ red pepper, de-seeded and sliced
1 tomato, chopped
1–2 roughly chopped fresh coriander sprigs
calorie controlled cooking spray
2 eggs
salt and freshly ground black pepper

1 Put the lime juice, soy sauce, chilli sauce and 1 teaspoon water in a medium bowl. Stir to make a dressing. Add the carrots, beansprouts, cabbage, pepper, tomatoes and coriander to the bowl and toss everything together.
2 Heat a non stick frying pan with a base measurement of 20 cm (8 inches) and spray with the cooking spray. Beat the eggs in a bowl, season, then pour them into the frying pan. Tilt the pan to ensure the egg covers the whole base. Cook until just set.
3 Slide on to a plate, then spoon the salad on to half of it and flip over the other side to serve.

Try this To enjoy for dinner, cook 50 g (1¾ oz) dried medium egg noodles according to packet instructions, then toss with 1 teaspoon soy sauce and serve alongside, for an additional 6 ***ProPoints*** values per serving.

Mediterranean Penne Pasta

A colourful vegetable-rich pasta dish that can also be served cold.

Serves 4
6 *ProPoints* values per serving
23 *ProPoints* values per recipe
35 minutes in total
V

1 teaspoon olive oil
1 red onion, chopped
2 courgettes, chopped
1 yellow pepper, de-seeded and chopped
1 celery stick, chopped
225 g (8 oz) dried wholewheat pasta, such as penne
1 garlic clove, sliced
½–1 red chilli, de-seeded and chopped, to taste
150 ml (5 fl oz) hot vegetable stock
8 cherry tomatoes, halved
a few roughly torn fresh basil leaves
salt and freshly ground black pepper

1 Heat the oil in a non stick wok or large frying pan and cook the onion, courgettes, pepper and celery for 5–10 minutes until starting to turn golden at the edges.
2 Bring a large pan of water to the boil and cook the pasta following the timings on the pack.
3 Add the garlic and chilli to the vegetables and cook for 1 minute. Pour in the stock, add the tomatoes and simmer for 5 minutes.
4 Drain the pasta, then tip back into the pan, season, and stir in the vegetables and fresh basil. Spoon into bowls and serve immediately.

Try this Ring the changes next time round and add 125 g (4½ oz) mozzarella, sliced and then diced, and 15 g (½ oz) sliced black olives, for 8 ***ProPoints*** values per serving.

Open Mushroom Lasagne

This is a clever way of making a quick lasagne without reheating everything in the oven. The lasagne and creamy sauce are cooked separately, then layered up in a free-form style together at the end.

Serves 2
8 *ProPoints* values per serving
16 *ProPoints* values per recipe
30 minutes in total
V

calorie controlled cooking spray
2 shallots, sliced finely
250 g (9 oz) chestnut mushrooms, sliced
1 garlic clove, crushed
4 dried lasagne sheets
150 ml (5 fl oz) hot vegetable stock
50 g (1¾ oz) spinach leaves
100 g (3½ oz) half fat crème fraîche
25 g (1 oz) Parmesan cheese
a few leaves of fresh basil or rocket
salt and freshly ground black pepper

1 Spray a non stick, lidded, medium frying pan with the cooking spray and cook the shallots and mushrooms, covered, for around 5 minutes until golden. Add a splash of water if the vegetables start to stick. Stir in the garlic and season well.

2 While the mushrooms are cooking, bring a large pan of water to the boil and cook the lasagne sheets according to packet instructions.

3 Pour the stock into the mushrooms and simmer, covered, for 5 minutes, then stir in the spinach and crème fraîche and season. Drain the lasagne sheets and cut each in half to make eight rough squares altogether.

4 Put one square of lasagne on each plate, then spoon some of the mixture on top. Add another square of lasagne and continue to layer up, alternating with the mushroom mixture until you have four layers of lasagne sheets and three layers of the mushroom mixture. Top with the Parmesan cheese and basil or rocket, and sprinkle over some black pepper. Serve immediately.

Baked Pepper Eggs

Roasted peppers and baked eggs are a winning and economical combination in this pretty supper dish.

Serves 2
5 ProPoints values per serving
10 ProPoints values per recipe
25 minutes in total
V

calorie controlled cooking spray
2 large roasted peppers, de-seeded if necessary,
    and cut into strips (see Cook's tip)
2 large eggs
100 g (3½ oz) half fat crème fraîche
2 tablespoons skimmed milk
1 tablespoon chopped fresh tarragon
salt and freshly ground black pepper

1 Preheat the oven to Gas Mark 4/180°C/fan oven 160°C. Spray the inside of two 150 ml (5 fl oz) large ramekin dishes with the cooking spray. Cut the peppers into thick strips and use to line the base and sides of the ramekins.
2 Crack an egg into each dish. Beat together the crème fraîche, milk, herb and seasoning. Spoon over the eggs and bake in the centre of the oven for 10 minutes or until lightly set. Serve immediately.

Cook's tips Cooking time will depend on the thickness of the dishes and the size of the eggs. To test, open the oven door and gently shake one of the ramekins, the egg should wobble slightly when done. Serve immediately as the egg will keep cooking with the heat of the dish.

Roasted peppers can be bought individually from the deli counter of most supermarkets, or found beside the pickles and chutneys in jars. To roast peppers at home, put in a roasting tin in a hot oven and roast for 20–25 minutes until soft and charred. Leave to cool for 10 minutes, then the skin will peel off easily. Remove the seeds.

Try this Spoon a teaspoon of Honeyed Red Onion Marmalade (see page 28) into the base of each ramekin before adding the egg for an extra 1 **ProPoints** value per serving.

Omelette and Spinach Cannelloni

Serve this light supper dish with a big crunchy salad such as a mixture of thinly sliced tomato, yellow pepper and chopped chives with a squeeze of lemon juice. The omelettes are really like very thin crepes.

Serves 2
4 ProPoints values per serving
8 ProPoints values per recipe
30 minutes in total
V

450 g (1 lb) spinach, washed
50 g (1¾ oz) low fat soft cheese
50 g (1¾ oz) Parmesan cheese, grated finely
a large pinch of grated nutmeg
2 eggs
calorie controlled cooking spray
salt and freshly ground black pepper

1 Put the spinach with the water clinging to the leaves into a large lidded saucepan, cover and cook for 6–7 minutes, or until tender. Drain well, squeezing out as much moisture as possible.
2 Add the soft cheese to the spinach along with half the Parmesan. Mix well and season with salt, pepper and grated nutmeg. Set aside.
3 Preheat the grill to medium high. Whisk the eggs with 1 tablespoon of water and season. Spray a small non stick frying pan with the cooking spray and heat, then pour in enough of the egg – about 2 tablespoons – to make a small, thin omelette. Move the pan around to allow the egg to form a thin layer. Cook for 30 seconds, until it is just set, then lift out on to a plate. Continue until you have made about 4–6 small omelettes.
4 Divide the spinach mixture between the omelettes, spooning it on to the edge of each one. Roll up the omelettes like cannelloni and place, side by side, in a shallow heatproof dish.
5 Sprinkle with the remaining Parmesan cheese and grill for about 5 minutes, or until bubbling and golden brown.

Cook's tip Make sure you squeeze as much moisture as possible from the cooked spinach. Leave it to cool for 1–2 minutes then squeeze with your hands till almost dry.

Roasted Onions with Sweet Potato

Bursting with flavour, these onions are perfect to prepare the day before, so they're ready to bake when needed.

Serves 4
4 *ProPoints* values per serving
14 *ProPoints* values per recipe
20 minutes preparation, 45 minutes cooking
V

4 large onions (about 200 g/7 oz each), peeled
calorie controlled cooking spray
1 or 2 fresh sage or rosemary leaves, or a pinch of dried
225 g (8 oz) sweet potato, peeled and diced
75 g (2¾ oz) green cabbage, shredded finely
250 ml (9 fl oz) vegetable stock
100 g (3½ oz) soft goat's cheese
4 tablespoons skimmed milk
freshly ground black pepper

1 Preheat the oven to Gas Mark 4/180°C/fan oven 160°C.
2 Cut the onions in half from root to tip. Pull out all but two layers from the centre of the onion to leave a thick shell and finely chop the inner layers. Cut a small slice from the rounded side of each onion shell so that they sit level. Spray a shallow non stick roasting tin with the cooking spray and sit the onion shells on the base. Bake in the oven for 10–15 minutes while you make the sweet potato hash.
3 Heat a non stick frying pan and spray with the cooking spray. Add the chopped onion and herb, and cook, stirring, for 5–7 minutes until the onion is beginning to soften. Add a splash of stock if the onion begins to stick. Stir in the sweet potato and cook, stirring, over a high heat for 1–2 minutes. Add the cabbage with the vegetable stock and bring to the boil. Bubble the stock with the vegetables for 7–10 minutes until most of the stock has evaporated and the vegetables are very tender. Keep an eye on it as timing depends on the size of the pan.
4 Spoon the sweet potato mixture into the onion shells, piling it up high. Don't worry if some falls off into the roasting tin.
5 Beat the cheese and milk together until smooth and spoon over the onion filling. Season with plenty of black pepper and return to the oven for 20–30 minutes until golden brown.

Cook's tip Use red or white onions for this recipe. If using red, pick out the largest in the pile.

Mixed Bean Wrap

This easy recipe is just as good for lunch as for a light supper. Plus there's no cooking involved, so it can be on the table and ready to eat in no time.

Serves 4
7 *ProPoints* values per serving
29 *ProPoints* values per recipe
15 minutes in total
V

½ x 400 g can of mixed beans in water, drained and rinsed
4 tablespoons ready-made tomato salsa
50 g (1¾ oz) half fat Cheddar cheese, grated
2 spring onions, chopped lengthways
4 x 60 g (2 oz) tortilla wraps
150 g (5½ oz) carrots, peeled and grated
25 g (1 oz) baby leaf spinach, chopped roughly
4 tablespoons 0% fat Greek yogurt
salt and freshly ground black pepper

1 Put the beans, tomato salsa, cheese and spring onions together in a bowl. Stir everything together and season.
2 Place the wraps on plates and divide the carrots and spinach equally between them. Spoon over the bean mixture, top each with 1 tablespoon yogurt then fold up each side of the wrap and turn up one end to enclose the filling. Serve immediately.

Wraps are quick and easy and you can fill them with almost anything you like.

Sweet Potato Patties with Chilli Salsa

Serves 4

9 *ProPoints* values per serving

36 *ProPoints* values per recipe

30 minutes preparation, 20 minutes cooking + chilling

V ✳

350 g (12 oz) sweet potato, *peeled and diced*

4 spring onions, *chopped finely*

1 garlic clove, *crushed*

1 cm (½ inch) fresh root ginger, *grated finely*

200 g (7 oz) dried brown basmati rice

1 teaspoon ground turmeric

calorie controlled cooking spray

salt and freshly ground black pepper

For the chilli salsa

½ red chilli, *de-seeded and chopped finely*

1 small avocado, peeled and diced

juice of a lime

a small handful of finely chopped fresh coriander

1 Put the sweet potato, spring onion, garlic and ginger in a steamer basket or metal sieve over a saucepan of boiling water. Cover with a lid or foil and steam for 20 minutes until very soft. Leave to cool. (Alternatively, cover with clingfilm and cook in a microwave on high for 4 minutes until very tender.)

2 Cook the basmati rice according to packet instructions, adding the turmeric to the cooking water. Drain well and leave to cool.

3 Mash together the sweet potato mixture with the spiced rice until well mixed. Season to taste. Shape into eight chunky patties and chill for 30 minutes.

4 Meanwhile, mix together all the salsa ingredients. Cover and set aside.

5 Spray the patties with the cooking spray. Heat a griddle pan or non stick frying pan until very hot, add half the patties and cook for 2–3 minutes on each side or until golden brown and hot through. Put on a plate and cover with foil to keep hot. Cook the remaining patties. Serve hot, with the salsa.

Cook's tip The uncooked patties freeze well so make a batch and keep some for another day. Defrost overnight in the fridge when you want to use them.

Fusilli with Light Spring Vegetables

This dish is simple to make, yet packed with the flavour and goodness of a range of green vegetables. It's best to cook it when the asparagus is in season during May and June for the best price, but if it's out of season increase the quantity of the green beans or spring onions instead.

Serves 4

7 *ProPoints* values per serving

30 *ProPoints* values per recipe

15 minutes in total

V

1 litre (1¾ pints) vegetable stock

225 g (8 oz) dried fusilli pasta

100 g (3½ oz) asparagus, *woody stem removed and sliced on the diagonal (optional)*

4 spring onions, *sliced finely*

100 g (3½ oz) frozen peas, *thawed*

100 g (3½ oz) frozen broad beans, *thawed*

100 g (3½ oz) French beans, *chopped roughly*

100 g (3½ oz) low fat soft cheese

zest of ½ a lemon

6 roughly torn fresh basil *leaves*

salt and freshly ground black pepper

1 Bring a large saucepan of stock to the boil. Add the pasta and cook according to packet instructions.

2 About 3–4 minutes before the end of the cooking time, add the vegetables and continue to cook until tender. Drain the pasta and vegetables, leaving about 100 ml (3½ fl oz) stock in the pan, then tip the mixture back in.

3 Place the pan back on the heat and stir in the low fat soft cheese, lemon zest and basil. Season well and serve.

Pinto and Pumpkin Casserole

This easy South American stew recipe is a cinch to make – and you can use any winter squash available.

Serves 4

6 *ProPoints* values per serving

23 *ProPoints* values per recipe

20 minutes preparation, 30 minutes cooking

V

750 g (1 lb 10 oz) **pumpkin** or **butternut squash**, *peeled, de-seeded and chopped*

2 **garlic cloves**, *crushed*

850 ml (1½ pints) vegetable stock

calorie controlled cooking spray

2 large **onions**, preferably red, chopped finely

2 large red, yellow or orange **peppers**, de-seeded and diced

a small handful of **fresh basil** leaves, chopped finely

150 g (5½ oz) frozen **sweetcorn**

2 x 400 g cans **pinto beans in water**, drained and rinsed

juice of a lemon

salt and freshly ground black pepper

a small handful of roughly chopped **fresh parsley** leaves, to serve

1 Put the pieces of pumpkin into a large saucepan with the garlic and stock. Bring to the boil, cover and simmer for about 15 minutes, or until the pumpkin is very tender. Whizz the contents of the pan to a thin purée using a hand blender. Tip into a bowl and set aside.

2 Rinse out the saucepan and spray with the cooking spray. Add the onions, peppers and basil and spray again with the cooking spray. Fry the vegetables over a medium heat for 7–10 minutes or until the onions are soft and slightly caramelised.

3 Return the pumpkin purée to the pan, and add the sweetcorn and beans. Simmer gently for 4–5 minutes until hot, add the lemon juice and season to taste. Serve in bowls, sprinkled with chopped parsley.

Spanish Stew

Serves 4

5 *ProPoints* values per serving

21 *ProPoints* values per recipe

35 minutes preparation + overnight soaking,
  1 hour cooking

V

125 g (4½ oz) dried **haricot beans**, *soaked in cold water overnight*

1 **fresh rosemary** sprig

1 bay leaf

calorie controlled cooking spray

1 **onion**, sliced

½ teaspoon paprika, or to taste

½ teaspoon crushed chilli flakes, or to taste

375 g (13 oz) **sweet potato**, peeled and chopped

1 red **pepper**, de-seeded and chopped

2 **celery** sticks, chopped

1 tablespoon tomato purée

1 vegetable stock cube

150 g (5½ oz) **green beans**, chopped

250 g (9 oz) **courgette**, chopped

1 tablespoon chopped **fresh parsley**

1 Drain the haricot beans and place in a lidded pan. Cover with plenty of cold water and add the rosemary and bay leaf. Cover, bring to the boil, then turn the heat right down low and simmer for 45 minutes, or until tender.

2 When the beans have cooked, drain them, reserving 600 ml (20 fl oz) of the cooking liquid, topping up with water if needed. Discard the rosemary and bay leaf.

3 Spray a medium pan with the cooking spray and place over a medium heat. Cook the onion for 5–10 minutes until just beginning to turn golden. Stir in the paprika and chilli flakes, sweet potato, red pepper and celery and continue to cook for 2–3 minutes.

4 Add the reserved cooking liquor, tomato purée, the stock cube and haricot beans and bring to the boil. Turn down the heat, cover, and simmer for 15 minutes until the sweet potato has softened.

5 Stir in the green beans and courgette and cook for 3–5 minutes until just tender. Scatter over the parsley, stir everything together, then ladle into bowls and serve.

Try this Dice 25 g (1 oz) chorizo sausage and dry-fry in a non stick frying pan until crisp. Drain any fat and add the chorizo at step 5 with the parsley for 6 ***ProPoints*** values per serving.

Vegetable Medley with Creamy Mushrooms

Add a 50 g (1¾ oz) crusty brown bread roll and a colourful salad of spinach, thinly sliced tomatoes, cucumber and red onion. Toss with a dressing of 1 teaspoon each of honey, olive oil and mustard with 1 tablespoon of lemon juice for an extra **6 ProPoints** values per serving.

Serves 4
2 ProPoints values per serving
9 ProPoints values per recipe
45 minutes in total
V

1 vegetable stock cube
750 g (1 lb 10 oz) white cabbage, cored and cut into fine strands
calorie controlled cooking spray
1 leek, sliced thinly
200 g (7 oz) chestnut mushrooms, sliced thinly
1 large garlic clove, crushed
a small handful of fresh chives, chopped finely
75 g (2¾ oz) frozen peas
75 g (2¾ oz) low fat soft cheese with garlic and herbs
150 ml (5 fl oz) skimmed milk
60 g (2 oz) half fat crème fraîche
salt and freshly ground black pepper

1 Half-fill a large saucepan with water and bring to the boil. Crumble in the stock cube and add the cabbage and cook, uncovered, for 5–6 minutes, or until tender. Cover and set aside to keep it warm in the heat of the stock.
2 Heat a medium size, non stick saucepan and spray with the cooking spray. Add the leek, mushrooms and garlic and cook for 2 minutes, stirring regularly. Stir in the chives and peas. Cook, stirring, for another 3 minutes.
3 Add the soft cheese, milk and crème fraîche. Season, and cook for a minute until hot.
4 Drain the cabbage and return to the saucepan. Stir the creamy mushroom mixture into the hot cabbage and serve immediately.

Cook's tip The sauce can be made ahead and kept in the fridge until needed. Stir through the hot cabbage until piping hot.

Stuffed Courgettes

Stir-fried, roasted or lightly steamed, these Mediterranean vegetables are incredibly versatile. Serve with a tomato salad, drizzled with a little balsamic vinegar, for no additional **ProPoints** values.

Serves 4
4 ProPoints values per serving
16 ProPoints values per recipe
20 minutes preparation, 40 minutes cooking
V

100 g (3½ oz) dried couscous
400 ml (14 fl oz) hot vegetable stock
4 large courgettes, about 350 g (12 oz) each, halved lengthways
4 spring onions, chopped
calorie controlled cooking spray
2 tablespoons chopped fresh chives or basil, plus extra to garnish
75 g (2¾ oz) half fat Cheddar cheese, grated
salt and freshly ground black pepper

1 Preheat the oven to Gas Mark 6/200°C/fan oven 180°C. Put the couscous in a bowl and pour over 100 ml (3½ fl oz) stock. Cover and set aside.
2 Run a spoon down the length of the courgettes to remove the seeds and some of the flesh. Roughly chop this and put it in a medium saucepan with the spring onions. Spray with the cooking spray and cook for around 10 minutes. Stir in the herb and season the mixture. Fluff up the couscous with a fork and stir it into this mixture with a third of the cheese.
3 Put the courgettes in a large ovenproof dish (25 x 35 x 6 cm/ 10 x 14 x 2½ inches) and spoon the filling inside. Pour the remaining stock around the courgettes, then spray the courgettes with the cooking spray. Cover with foil and bake in the oven for 30 minutes until the courgettes are tender.
4 Remove the foil, sprinkle over the remaining cheese and return to the oven, uncovered, for about 10 minutes, until the cheese is golden.

At the photo shoot, these yummy courgettes were a real hit and disappeared quickly.

Japanese Tofu Noodles

Full of texture and colour, this filling main course combines exciting flavours to make a really delicious family meal that won't break your budget.

Serves 4

8 ProPoints values per serving

33 ProPoints values per recipe

45 minutes in total + marinating

V

125 g (4½ oz) broccoli florets, sliced thinly

1 carrot, peeled and pared into thin strips
  using a vegetable peeler

100 g (3½ oz) chestnut mushrooms,
  sliced thinly

200 g (7 oz) fine dried egg noodles

calorie controlled cooking spray

100 g (3½ oz) sugar snap peas

2 spring onions, sliced diagonally

¼ red chilli, de-seeded and sliced thinly

1.2 litres (2 pints) vegetable stock

a sachet of miso paste

a handful of fresh coriander, chopped

For the tofu

2.5 cm (1 inch) fresh root ginger,
  peeled and grated

½ teaspoon light muscovado sugar

5 tablespoons light soy sauce

300 g (10½ oz) firm tofu, cut into 5 mm
  (¼ inch) slices

1 Start with the tofu. Put the ginger and sugar in a shallow dish with 2 tablespoons of soy sauce. Toss the tofu pieces in the mixture and leave to marinate for as long as you can, at least 30 minutes but preferably overnight.

2 Bring a large saucepan of water to the boil, add the broccoli and carrot, cook for 2 minutes then add the mushrooms. Cook for 1 minute then add the noodles. Return to the boil and cook for another 2–3 minutes until tender. Drain and refresh under cold water. Set aside.

3 Drain the tofu, reserving any marinade. Heat a wok or large non stick frying pan and spray with the cooking spray. Fry the tofu, a few pieces at a time, on both sides, for about 1 minute on each side. Remove from the pan and set aside.

4 Wipe the pan with kitchen paper, spray again with the cooking spray and stir-fry the sugar snap peas, spring onion and chilli for 2 minutes.

5 Meanwhile, heat the stock in a saucepan then stir in the miso paste, remaining soy sauce and any reserved marinade.

6 Divide the noodles, tofu and vegetables between four large bowls. Pour over the stock then sprinkle over the coriander.

Try this You could swap the tofu for the same weight of skinless turkey breast strips. Marinate and stir-fry as in step 3 for the same **ProPoints** values per serving.

Three Veg Fritters with Poached Egg

The sweet flavours of carrot, courgette and beetroot combine in this colourful fritter.

Serves 2
3 *ProPoints* values per serving
6 *ProPoints* values per recipe
45 minutes in total
V

150 g (5½ oz) carrots, *peeled and grated*
225 g (8 oz) courgettes, *grated*
75 g (2¾ oz) beetroot, *grated*
3 eggs
1 red chilli, *de-seeded and chopped (or to taste)*
1 tablespoon chopped fresh parsley
calorie controlled cooking spray
salt and freshly ground black pepper

1 Squeeze the grated carrots, courgettes and beetroot through dry kitchen towel to remove any excess liquid. Beat one of the eggs in a bowl, then add the carrots, courgettes, chilli, parsley and beetroot. Season.
2 Spray a medium size, non stick frying pan with the cooking spray and place over a medium heat. Divide the mixture roughly into six, then form each portion into a round patty. Fry in batches on each side for 2–3 minutes until golden. If necessary, spray the pan again when you turn the patties over. Continue to cook the remaining portions.
3 Meanwhile, bring a medium lidded pan quarter-filled with water to the boil. Turn down to a simmer. Crack each egg into a cup, then gently tip into the water one at a time and allow to poach gently, covered. Cook for 3 minutes, then remove carefully with a slotted spoon. Rest the spoon briefly on a pad of kitchen paper to remove any excess water.
4 Put three patties on each plate and top with a poached egg.

Cook's tip Fresh parsley or a little rocket makes a delicious garnish on top of this dish.

Simple Lentil Dal

This is easy to make and a warming, nourishing supper for a cold night.

Serves 4
11 *ProPoints* values per serving
42 *ProPoints* values per recipe
20 minutes preparation, 30 minutes cooking
V ✳

calorie controlled cooking spray
½ onion, *grated*
1 garlic clove, *crushed*
75 g (2¾ oz) chana dal *or* yellow split peas, *rinsed*
125 g (4½ oz) *dried red* lentils, *rinsed*
600 ml (20 fl oz) hot vegetable stock
½ teaspoon mustard seeds
½ teaspoon cumin seeds
2 tomatoes, *chopped finely*
4 teaspoons virtually fat free plain yogurt
4 x 60 g (2 oz) wholemeal flatbreads
salt and freshly ground black pepper

1 Spray a large lidded pan with the cooking spray and cook the onion for 5 minutes until starting to turn golden. Stir in the garlic and cook for 1 minute.
2 Add the chana dal or split peas, the lentils and the stock. Cover with a lid and cook over a low heat for 20–30 minutes until thickened.
3 Spray a non stick frying pan with the cooking spray and cook the mustard and cumin seeds until the mustard seeds start to pop and the spices smell fragrant. Add the tomato and continue to cook for 1 minute to warm the tomato through. Season.
4 Divide the dal between bowls, top with the tomato mixture and yogurt and serve the flatbread alongside.

Moroccan Aubergines

The rich flavour of aubergines provides the perfect foil for a lightly spiced lentil stew.

Serves 4

3 *ProPoints* values per serving

12 *ProPoints* values per recipe

20 minutes preparation,
   30 minutes cooking

V

4 aubergines, *halved*

1 teaspoon olive oil

1 onion, *chopped finely*

2 celery *sticks, chopped finely*

1 garlic clove, *crushed*

1 teaspoon ground cumin

1 teaspoon ground coriander

¼ teaspoon chilli flakes

400 g can chopped tomatoes

100 g (3½ oz) dried red lentils, *rinsed*

300 ml (10 fl oz) hot vegetable stock

salt and freshly ground black pepper

To garnish

50 g (1¾ oz) 0% fat Greek yogurt

1 tablespoon fresh parsley *or*
   coriander *leaves*

1 Preheat the oven to Gas Mark 6/200°C/fan oven 180°C. Score the aubergine halves then put on a baking sheet and brush or spray with ½ teaspoon oil. Roast for 30 minutes until tender.

2 Heat the remaining oil in a medium size lidded pan and fry the onion and celery for around 5 minutes until just golden. Stir in the garlic and spices and cook for 1 minute.

3 Add the tomatoes, lentils and stock and season, then stir briefly and cover. Bring to the boil, then turn the heat down low and cook for 20 minutes.

4 Put the aubergines on plates, spoon over the stew, then garnish with the yogurt and parsley.

Fish & Seafood

Fabulous fish, whether fresh, frozen or tinned, can often be the smart cook's best friend.

Parmesan Fish Pastries

These crispy fish pastries go well with steamed spinach and 50 g (1¾ oz) boiled new potatoes per person, for an additional 1 *ProPoints* value per serving.

Serves 4

4 *ProPoints* values per serving

16 *ProPoints* values per recipe

15 minutes preparation,
   20 minutes cooking

4 x 100 g (3½ oz) thick pieces white fish fillet

50 g (1¾ oz) low fat soft cheese with chives

1 tablespoon skimmed milk

45 g sheet Jus-Rol filo pastry, measuring
   50 x 24 cm (20 x 9½ inches), defrosted
   if frozen

calorie controlled cooking spray

10 g (¼ oz) sunflower seeds (see Cook's tip)

25 g (1 oz) Parmesan cheese, grated finely

freshly ground black pepper

1 Preheat the oven to Gas Mark 6/200°C/fan oven 180°C.

2 Place the fish pieces on a non stick baking sheet. Beat the soft cheese and milk together and then season well with black pepper.

3 Spread the top of each piece of fish with a little of the cheese mixture.

4 Roll up the filo pastry and, with a sharp knife or scissors, cut into thin ribbons. Spray the pastry with the cooking spray and toss with the seeds if using, and half the Parmesan cheese.

5 Sprinkle the cheesy pastry strips over each piece of fish and sprinkle with the remaining cheese.

6 Bake in the oven for 15–20 minutes or until the fish is just cooked and the pastry is golden and crisp. Serve immediately.

Cook's tips When using filo pastry, allow plenty of time for thawing if it is frozen. Always keep the pastry covered with a clean tea towel before using, as it dries out quickly.

You could use the remaining sunflower seeds from the packet for salads, to add texture and extra flavour. Remember to add the extra *ProPoints* values.

Try this Swap the soft cheese for a soft goat's cheese and 3 finely chopped stoned black olives for 5 *ProPoints* values per serving.

Crispy Fillets with Roasted Garlic Sauce

This fish dish of crispy golden crumbed fillets couldn't be easier. The sauce will keep, covered, in the fridge for 3–4 days. Serve with 50 g (1¾ oz) dried brown basmati rice per person, cooked according to packet instructions, and steamed spring greens or broccoli, for an additional 5 *ProPoints* values per serving.

Serves 4
4 *ProPoints* values per serving
15 *ProPoints* values per recipe
45 minutes in total

2 tablespoons dried fine polenta
4 x 100 g (3½ oz) thick fillets of white fish
    (such as pollock)
salt and freshly ground black pepper
lemon wedges, to serve

For the roasted garlic sauce
½ bulb of garlic, about 6 cloves
calorie controlled cooking spray
1 tablespoon chopped fresh basil
40 g (1½ oz) extra light mayonnaise
150 g pot 0% fat Greek yogurt
4 tablespoons skimmed milk

1 Preheat the oven to Gas Mark 6/200°C/fan oven 180°C.
2 First make the roasted garlic sauce. Put the garlic cloves (no need to peel) in a small ovenproof dish and spray with the cooking spray. Roast in the oven for 15–20 minutes or until golden and soft. Push the soft garlic flesh from the skins.
3 Using a whisk, beat the garlic together with all the remaining sauce ingredients. Season to taste, cover and set aside.
4 Preheat the grill to high. Line a grill pan with foil. Put the polenta on a flat plate and season. Spray the fish pieces on one side only with the cooking spray and dip that side into the polenta to coat. Put the fish on the grill pan, polenta side up, and spray again with the cooking spray.
5 Grill the fish, without turning, for 4–5 minutes, or until golden brown and cooked through.
6 Serve the fish with the roasted garlic sauce and lemon wedges to squeeze over.

Roasted Fish with Bean Mash

This quick fish recipe looks as impressive as top restaurant food but is very simple to make. Serve with the mash and Oven-roasted Ratatouille (see page 32).

Serves 4
6 *ProPoints* values per serving
25 *ProPoints* values per recipe
15 minutes preparation, 20 minutes cooking

calorie controlled cooking spray
4 x 100 g (3½ oz) thick white fish fillets (such as pollock)
4 slices prosciutto ham
12 cherry tomatoes or 4 tomatoes, halved horizontally
juice of a lemon
salt and freshly ground black pepper
lemon wedges, to serve

For the bean and parsley mash
225 g (8 oz) potatoes, peeled and diced
400 g can butter beans in water, drained and rinsed
75 g (2¾ oz) half fat crème fraîche
1 tablespoon chopped fresh parsley

1 Preheat the oven to Gas Mark 6/200°C/fan oven 180°C.
2 Spray the base of a shallow roasting tin with the cooking spray. Wrap each fish fillet with one slice of prosciutto ham. Put seam side down in the roasting tin and spray with the cooking spray. Scatter the tomatoes around the fish and spoon over about 1 tablespoon of lemon juice then season everything with plenty of ground black pepper. Roast in the oven for 15–20 minutes, depending on thickness.
3 Meanwhile, put the potatoes in a medium saucepan and cover in cold water, bring up to the boil, then reduce the heat and simmer for 15–20 minutes or until very tender. Drain and mash to a rough mash with the butter beans and the crème fraîche, seasoning and remaining lemon juice, to taste. Put in a small non stick saucepan and heat gently, stirring, over a medium heat until piping hot. Stir in the parsley and serve with the roasted fish and roasted tomatoes with some lemon wedges to squeeze over the top.

Cook's tip The fish can be wrapped in ham the day before, ready to roast.

Lemony Linguine with Trout

Make a little luxury go a long way with this economical and tasty smoked trout pasta supper.

Serves 2
11 *ProPoints* values per serving
22 *ProPoints* values per recipe
20 minutes in total

1 vegetable stock cube, crumbled
125 g (4½ oz) dried linguine
125 g pack smoked trout fillets,
    flaked into bite size chunks

For the lemon and rosemary sauce

calorie controlled cooking spray
1 onion, chopped finely
1 garlic clove, crushed or sliced
1 teaspoon finely chopped fresh rosemary
¼ red chilli, de-seeded and chopped finely
grated zest of ½ a lemon
1 teaspoon cornflour
90 g (3¼ oz) half fat crème fraîche
freshly ground black pepper

1 Bring a pan of water to the boil, add the vegetable stock cube and the pasta and cook for 7–10 minutes or according to the packet instructions.

2 Meanwhile, to make the lemon and rosemary sauce, heat a small saucepan and spray with the cooking spray. Add the onion, garlic, rosemary, chilli and lemon zest and cook, stirring, for 4–5 minutes until softened. Add a splash of water if the onions begin to stick.

3 Drain the pasta when cooked, reserving 150 ml (5 fl oz) of the pasta cooking liquid and then return the pasta to the pan. Add the cooking liquid to the onion mixture then bring to the boil. Blend the cornflour to a smooth paste with a little of the cooking liquid and whisk into the onion mixture. Simmer gently for 1–2 minutes until lightly thickened. Reduce the heat and stir in the crème fraîche and plenty of black pepper to finish making the sauce.

4 Stir the sauce into the pasta. Reheat gently and then serve in heated bowls, topped with the flaked smoked trout.

Cook's tip The lemon and rosemary sauce is also excellent with steamed fish, or skinless boneless chicken breast.

Try this Swap the smoked trout for the same weight of cooked, peeled prawns for 10 *ProPoints* values per serving.

V For a vegetarian alternative, omit the trout and add 125 g (4½ oz) Quorn pieces to the fried onion mixture in step 3 after adding the cornflour for 10 *ProPoints* values per serving.

Thai Fish Cakes

A tasty way to cook fish and an ideal make ahead meal that can be cooked in minutes once chilled. Serve with some steamed pak choi and 60 g (2 oz) dried brown basmati rice per person, cooked according to packet instructions, for an extra 6 *ProPoints* values per serving.

Serves 4
4 *ProPoints* values per serving
16 *ProPoints* values per recipe
20 minutes preparation, 15 minutes cooking + chilling

calorie controlled cooking spray
lime wedges, to serve

For the fish cakes
600 g (1 lb 5 oz) white fish *fillet (such as* pollock*), chopped very finely*
a bunch of spring onions*, chopped finely*
a handful of roughly chopped fresh coriander
40 g (1½ oz) red Thai curry paste
finely grated zest and juice of a lime
1 large egg white

For the dipping sauce
juice of ½ a lime
2 tablespoons light soy sauce
1 teaspoon chopped fresh mint *or* fresh coriander
2 teaspoons honey

1 Make the dipping sauce by stirring all the ingredients together in a small bowl until the honey dissolves. Cover and chill overnight.
2 Beat together all the ingredients for the fish cakes. Cover and chill overnight. With slightly wet hands shape the mixture into four fish cakes. Place on a baking sheet or large flat plate, cover and chill again for at least 1 hour.
3 Preheat the grill to high. Line the grill pan with foil and spray with the cooking spray. Place the fish cakes on the tray and spray with the cooking spray.
4 Cook the fish cakes under the grill, turning frequently, for about 15 minutes, until golden brown all over and cooked through. Serve with the dipping sauce and lime wedges.

Cook's tip Using a hand blender with a goblet, you can whizz together all the ingredients for the fish cakes in seconds.

Try this Use 300 g (10½ oz) white fish fillet and 300 g (10½ oz) cooked, peeled prawns for 4 *ProPoints* values per serving.

Mackerel Fillets with Fennel Slaw

The slightly acidic dressing is a perfect match for oily mackerel fillets and makes this a great light meal.

Serves 2
8 *ProPoints* values per serving
16 *ProPoints* values per recipe
20 minutes in total

2 x 100 g (3½ oz) skinless fresh mackerel fillets
calorie controlled cooking spray
salt and freshly ground black pepper

For the fennel slaw
100 g (3½ oz) fennel*, sliced thinly,*
   any feathery green tops reserved
125 g (4½ oz) cucumber*, sliced thinly*
½ a small onion *or shallot, sliced thinly*
100 g (3½ oz) radishes*, sliced thinly*

For the dressing
2 teaspoons white wine vinegar
1 teaspoon Dijon mustard
1 teaspoon mustard seeds (optional)
2 teaspoons clear honey
30 g (1¼ oz) half fat crème fraîche
1 tablespoon lemon juice

1 Mix together all the dressing ingredients in a large bowl and season.
2 Add the fennel, cucumber, onion and radishes to the bowl and turn to coat in the dressing.
3 Preheat the grill to hot. Line the grill pan with foil and place the mackerel fillets on top. Finely chop the feathery green fennel tops and sprinkle over the mackerel. Spray with the cooking spray, season with plenty of black pepper and grill the fillets for 4–5 minutes, without turning, until cooked through. Serve with the Fennel Slaw.

Try this For a complete meal in a bowl, swap the mackerel for 100 g (3½ oz) cooked, peeled prawns per person for 4 *ProPoints* values per serving, or add 220 g (7½ oz) flaked cooked salmon per person and stir lightly through the Fennel Slaw before serving for 8 *ProPoints* values per serving.

Mackerel is a deliciously rich and satisfying fish and this recipe makes the most of its fabulous flavour.

Cheesy Cod with Olives

One of the great things about fish is how speedy it is to cook. This delicious dish can be prepared and on the table in 30 minutes.

Serves 4
4 ProPoints values per serving
16 ProPoints values per recipe
30 minutes in total

1 x 20 g (¾ oz) slice Weight Watchers Sliced Brown
    Danish Bread
4 x 100 g (3½ oz) chunky cod loins
1 roasted red pepper, chopped very finely (see Cook's tip)
8 stoned black olives, chopped finely
1 teaspoon capers in brine, drained
125 g pack light mozzarella cheese, sliced thinly
calorie controlled cooking spray
freshly ground black pepper

1 Preheat the grill to high and line the grill pan with foil. Coarsely grate the bread into rough breadcrumbs. Put the cod on the grill pan and season with plenty of black pepper. Cook the cod for 1–2 minutes on one side.
2 Divide the roasted pepper between the cod pieces. Sprinkle with the chopped black olives and capers.
3 Lay the mozzarella on top of the fish. Sprinkle with the breadcrumbs, spray with the cooking spray and pop the fish back under the grill for 7–10 minutes until the cheese is golden brown and bubbling. Serve immediately.

Cook's tips Roasted peppers can be bought from the deli counter of most supermarkets. They are also available in jars and will keep in the fridge for a couple of weeks after opening.

To roast fresh peppers, put them in a roasting tin in a hot oven and roast for 20–25 minutes until soft and charred. Leave to cool for 10 minutes. The skin will peel off easily. Remove the seeds.

Try this Swap the sliced mozzarella for thin slices of the same weight of half fat Cheddar cheese for 5 **ProPoints** values per serving.

Smoky Seafood Stew

A rustic yet sophisticated seafood stew that will be a winner with both family and friends. Serve with a simple mixed green salad of soft round lettuce leaves plus a 40 g (1½ oz) slice of brown Irish soda bread for an extra 2 **ProPoints** values per serving.

Serves 4
5 ProPoints values per serving
19 ProPoints values per recipe
15 minutes preparation, 30 minutes cooking

calorie controlled cooking spray
1 large onion, chopped
1 garlic clove, crushed
3 peppers, de-seeded and chopped
3 courgettes, chopped roughly
2 teaspoons smoked paprika
2 strips pared orange zest and the juice of an orange
¼ red chilli (optional)
2 x 400 g cans chopped tomatoes
125 ml (4 fl oz) dry white wine
225 ml (8 fl oz) vegetable stock
400 g can butter beans in water, drained and rinsed
400 g bag frozen mixed seafood (fruits de mer), defrosted
a small handful of chopped fresh parsley, to serve

1 Heat a large saucepan and spray with the cooking spray. Add the onions and garlic and cook, stirring, for about 6 minutes or until softened. Stir in the pepper, courgette and paprika and continue to cook, stirring, for 1–2 minutes.
2 Add the orange zest and juice, chilli, if using, tomatoes, wine and stock. Bring to the boil then reduce the heat and simmer gently for about 30 minutes or until all the vegetables are tender.
3 Stir in the butter beans and seafood and simmer for a further 3–4 minutes, just long enough to heat through. Serve in bowls, sprinkled with parsley.

Cook's tip If you don't have any smoked paprika, simple ground paprika will be just as good.

V Try this For a vegetarian alternative, swap the seafood for the same quantity of halved chestnut mushrooms. Simmer in the stew for 10–15 minutes. The **ProPoints** values will be 3 per serving.

Two leeks could be used instead of the courgettes, if you prefer.

Spiced Rice and Seafood Bowl

This filling and budget-friendly supper is a complete meal in itself.

Serves 4
8 _ProPoints_ values per serving
31 _ProPoints_ values per recipe
30 minutes in total

225 g (8 oz) dried long grain brown rice
100 g (3½ oz) frozen peas
calorie controlled cooking spray
1 small leek, sliced
1 spring onion, chopped
2 garlic cloves, crushed
25 g (1 oz) mild tikka spice paste
½ x 400 g bag frozen mixed seafood (fruits de mer), defrosted
finely grated zest and juice of ½ a lemon
salt and freshly ground black pepper
a small handful of chopped fresh flat leaf parsley, to serve

1 Bring a large saucepan of water to the boil. Add the rice and cook according to packet instructions until just tender. Add the frozen peas for the last 1–2 minutes of cooking time. Drain and rinse under cold water then drain again.
2 Heat a wok or large non stick frying pan. Spray with the cooking spray and stir-fry the leek, spring onion and garlic together for 3–4 minutes. Stir in the tikka paste and cook for a further minute.
3 Tip the rice and peas into the wok or frying pan and stir-fry over a medium heat for 1 minute. Add the seafood, lemon zest and juice and seasoning and cook for a further 1–2 minutes until everything is piping hot. Sprinkle with the parsley and serve immediately.

Try this Swap the mixed seafood for the same weight of cooked, peeled prawns, defrosted, for the same **_ProPoints_** values per serving.

Pappardelle Noodle Pot

One of the best 'meal in a pot' pasta dishes to suit all the family.

Serves 4
11 _ProPoints_ values per serving
46 _ProPoints_ values per recipe
30 minutes in total

250 g (9 oz) dried pappardelle pasta or spaghetti
calorie controlled cooking spray
4 spring onions, chopped
75 g (2¾ oz) frozen French or green beans
1 red pepper, de-seeded and sliced thinly
175 g (6 oz) frozen broad beans
150 g (5½ oz) half fat crème fraîche
50 g (1¾ oz) extra light mayonnaise
50 ml (2 fl oz) skimmed milk
finely grated zest of ½ a lemon
1 teaspoon cornflour
40 g (1½ oz) half fat Cheddar cheese, grated finely
120 g can tuna fish in spring water, drained
salt and freshly ground black pepper
1 tablespoon chopped fresh basil, plus a few leaves, to garnish

1 Cook the pasta according to packet instructions, until just tender.
2 Meanwhile, preheat the grill to medium high. Spray a large non stick frying pan or wok with the cooking spray. Add the spring onion, French beans and pepper. Stir-fry for 3–4 minutes then add the frozen broad beans. Cook, stirring, for a further 1–2 minutes.
3 Drain the pasta, reserving 6 tablespoons of the cooking liquid. Put the crème fraîche, mayonnaise, milk and lemon zest into a small saucepan. Mix the cornflour to a smooth paste with the reserved cooking liquid in a small bowl and stir into the pan with the crème fraîche mixture. Bring to the boil then simmer over a low heat until smooth and lightly thickened. Stir in half the cheese and season. Preheat the grill to high.
4 Tip the pasta, vegetables, flaked tuna, basil and sauce into a shallow heatproof dish. Sprinkle with the remaining grated cheese and grill until golden. Serve immediately, garnished with basil leaves.

V **Try this** Omit the tuna fish for an equally tasty vegetarian supper for the same **_ProPoints_** values.

Meat & Poultry

These recipe ideas make the most of simple ingredients to help you create meals the family will love.

Pork Polpette with Pepper Stew

Serve with 60 g (2 oz) dried rice or dried tagliatelle pasta per person, cooked according to packet instructions, for an extra 6 *ProPoints* values per serving.

Serves 4
5 *ProPoints* values per serving
20 *ProPoints* values per recipe
40 minutes preparation,
   35 minutes cooking
* meatballs only

1 teaspoon olive oil
2 onions, one sliced finely and one diced finely
1 red pepper, de-seeded and sliced finely
1 yellow pepper, de-seeded and sliced finely
1 orange pepper, de-seeded and sliced finely
1 medium slice bread
1 tablespoon each of chopped fresh thyme
   and fresh parsley, plus extra, to serve
250 g (9 oz) lean pork mince
1 egg yolk, beaten (see Cook's tip)
1–2 tablespoons plain flour
calorie controlled cooking spray
400 g can chopped tomatoes
200 ml (7 fl oz) hot chicken stock
salt and freshly ground black pepper

1 Heat the oil in a medium lidded saucepan and fry the sliced onion and peppers over a low to medium heat, covered, for around 20 minutes, stirring occasionally. Add a drizzle of water if the vegetables start to stick on the bottom.

2 Whizz together the bread, diced onion and herbs in a food processor or hand blender to make breadcrumbs. (You could also grate the bread, instead.) Tip into a bowl. Add the pork mince and egg yolk and season. Mix well, then shape into 20 mini meatballs, each around the size of a walnut. Sprinkle the flour on a plate and roll the meatballs lightly in the flour.

3 Spray a non stick frying pan with the cooking spray and heat until hot. Cook the meatballs in batches until golden all over. Meanwhile, stir the tomatoes and stock into the pepper mixture and continue to simmer, uncovered.

4 Drop the meatballs into the tomato mixture and simmer, covered, for 15 minutes until cooked through. Sprinkle over extra herbs to garnish, and serve.

Cook's tip You can use the egg white to make the Meringue and Ice Cream Peaches on page 96.

Turkey and Vegetables with Quinoa

Cooking the turkey and vegetables in a roasting bag is a clever way of sealing in all the flavour and produces a ready-made sauce.

Serves 4
8 ProPoints values per serving
30 ProPoints values per recipe
20 minutes preparation, 50 minutes cooking

500 g (1 lb 2 oz) **skinless boneless turkey breast**, *chopped into bite size pieces*
500 g (1 lb 2 oz) **butternut squash**, *peeled, de-seeded and chopped into bite size pieces*
1 red **onion**, *cut into wedges*
1 yellow **pepper**, *halved, de-seeded and cut into chunks*
½ **aubergine**, *chopped into bite size pieces*
1 chicken stock cube
zest of a lemon
½ teaspoon ground cumin
calorie controlled cooking spray
100 g (3½ oz) dried **quinoa**
400 g can **chick peas in water**, *drained and rinsed*
salt and freshly ground black pepper

1 Preheat the oven to Gas Mark 5/190°C/fan oven 170°C. Put a roasting bag in a roasting tin, then fill the bag with the turkey pieces, squash, red onion, pepper and aubergine.
2 Crumble the stock cube into a small bowl and add the lemon zest, ground cumin and seasoning. Stir together then tip into the roasting bag. Spray the contents of the bag with the cooking spray, then seal the bag and shake to coat all the ingredients in the zest and spice. Roast in the tin for 50 minutes.
3 About 15 minutes before the turkey mixture has finished cooking, cook the quinoa according to packet instructions.
4 Snip the roasting bag open and empty the contents into the roasting tin. Stir in the chick peas along with the quinoa and serve in bowls.

Chicken in the Pot

As the name suggests, this classic French dish cooks everything together and leaves enough leftover chicken to make two more meals.

Serves 4
5 ProPoints values per serving
52 ProPoints values per recipe
20 minutes preparation, 1 hour cooking

1.5 kg (3 lb 5 oz) whole chicken
1 **fresh bay leaf**
1 **fresh thyme** *sprig*
1 **onion**, *quartered*
2 **carrots**, *peeled and cut into chunks*
2 **celery** *sticks, cut into chunks, any green leaves reserved*
2.5 litres (4½ pints) chicken stock
100 g (3½ oz) **turnip**, *peeled and cut into bite size chunks*
250 g (9 oz) **swede**, *peeled and cut into bite size chunks*
75 g (2¾ oz) **broccoli** *florets, halved*
a small handful of chopped **fresh parsley**
freshly ground black pepper

1 Put the chicken on a board and remove all visible fat, checking especially inside the cavity. Remove the skin from the chicken using a sharp knife and then discard it.
2 Put the chicken in a large lidded pan with the bay leaf and thyme. Add the onion, carrots and celery sticks. Season with black pepper. Add the stock. Cover and bring to the boil over a medium heat. Once the stock is bubbling, turn down the heat to a simmer and cook for 45 minutes.
3 Add the turnip and swede and continue to cook for 15 minutes. Add the broccoli and cook for 3–5 minutes longer until tender. Lift the chicken out of the pan, making sure all the liquid runs back into the pan. Put on a warm plate. Stir the parsley into the vegetables and season with plenty of black pepper. Sprinkle with celery leaves, if desired.
4 Slice the chicken and serve 100 g (3½ oz) each in bowls. Spoon over the vegetables and some of the stock and serve.

Cook's tip Cool the chicken and take all the meat off the bone. Discard the bones. Use for the Open Chicken and Vegetable Sandwich (see page 70) or Chicken Spring Rolls (see page 71). The meat can be frozen for up to a month or it will keep in the fridge for up to 3 days.

Chicken with a Ginger and Orange Sauce

Serve with 60 g (2 oz) dried brown rice per person, cooked according to packet instructions, for an extra 6 *ProPoints* values per serving.

Serves 4
5 *ProPoints* values per serving
18 *ProPoints* values per recipe
25 minutes in total + 30 minutes marinating

4 x 150 g (5½ oz) skinless boneless chicken breasts
juice of 2 oranges
3 tablespoons red wine vinegar
1 garlic clove, *crushed*
1 cm (½ inch) fresh root ginger, *peeled and grated*
3 tablespoons soy sauce
2 teaspoons tomato ketchup
1 tablespoon honey
calorie controlled cooking spray

For the vegetables
250 g (9 oz) large courgettes, *sliced*
150 g (5½ oz) large carrots, *peeled and sliced*
200 g (7 oz) mange tout
200 g (7 oz) baby corn, *halved lengthways*
200 g (7 oz) green beans

1 Put the chicken breasts on a board and slice each in half horizontally to make eight thin escalopes.
2 Mix the orange juice, vinegar, garlic, ginger, soy sauce, ketchup and honey in a non metallic bowl and add the chicken. Toss to coat, then cover and marinate in the fridge for at least 30 minutes and up to 24 hours.
3 Spray a lidded non stick frying pan with the cooking spray and heat until hot. Add the chicken in batches, reserving the marinade, and cook for 3 minutes on one side. Turn over and continue to cook each batch for 3 minutes. Add all the chicken to the pan, then the marinade, cover and bring to a simmer. Cook over a low heat for 15–20 minutes until the chicken is cooked through.
4 Around 10 minutes before the chicken is cooked, cook the vegetables until just tender. Remove the chicken from the pan and put on a warm plate. Increase the heat for the sauce and simmer for 2 minutes to thicken slightly. Serve the chicken with the vegetables and the sauce spooned over.

Open Chicken and Vegetable Sandwich

This is an ideal lunch dish and uses up some of the leftover chicken from the Chicken in the Pot recipe on page 68.

Serves 4
7 *ProPoints* values per serving
28 *ProPoints* values per recipe
20 minutes preparation, 30 minutes cooking

calorie controlled cooking spray
1 aubergine, *cut into bite size pieces*
1 butternut squash, *peeled, de-seeded and cut into bite size pieces*
1 red pepper, *halved, de-seeded and cut into chunks*
1 red onion, *cut into wedges*
200 g (7 oz) ciabatta bread
75 g (2¾ oz) virtually fat free plain yogurt
juice of ½ a lemon
100 g (3½ oz) reduced fat houmous
100 g (3½ oz) skinless cooked chicken, shredded
salt and freshly ground black pepper
a handful of fresh basil *leaves, to garnish*

1 Preheat the oven to Gas Mark 7/220°C/fan oven 200°C. Spray a baking sheet with the cooking spray, put the chopped vegetables on top, season and spray again. Roast for 20–30 minutes until golden and starting to char at the edges. Check them halfway through cooking and move the vegetables around if they're colouring more on one side than another.
2 Remove the vegetables from the oven and turn on the grill to medium high. Cut the ciabatta in half lengthways, then cut each piece in half again to make four pieces. Toast lightly on the cut side. Put each on a plate.
3 Mix together the yogurt, lemon juice and houmous in a medium size bowl, then stir in the chicken and season. Spread a quarter over each piece of ciabatta. Top with the roasted vegetables and basil leaves and serve.

Chicken Spring Rolls

This is a great way to stretch a little bit of leftover shredded chicken to make another meal.

Serves 4
5 ProPoints values per serving
21 ProPoints values per recipe
20 minutes preparation,
   20 minutes cooking

calorie controlled cooking spray
½ **onion**, sliced very finely
2 **carrots**, peeled and cut into matchsticks
¼ white **cabbage**, shredded finely
½ red **chilli**, de-seeded and chopped finely
1 **garlic clove**, sliced very finely
1 cm (½ inch) **fresh root ginger**, peeled and
   cut into matchsticks
1 tablespoon soy sauce
125 g (4½ oz) skinless cooked chicken,
   shredded
4 x 45 g sheets Jus-Rol filo pastry, each
   measuring 50 x 24 cm (20 x 9½ inches),
   defrosted if frozen
½ teaspoon sesame seeds

To serve
2 tablespoons sweet chilli sauce
2 tablespoons soy sauce
½ **cucumber**, cut into matchsticks

1 Spray a non stick frying pan or wok with the cooking spray and fry the onion, carrots, cabbage, chilli, garlic and ginger in the pan with 1 tablespoon water. Cook for about 5 minutes until the edges of the vegetables start to turn golden, tossing every now and then. Stir in the soy sauce.

2 Tip the vegetables into a large bowl and spread out to cool quickly. Once cool, stir through the shredded chicken. Divide the mixture roughly into eight portions. Preheat the oven to Gas Mark 6/200°C/fan oven 180°C.

3 Take one filo sheet and lay it on a large board, so the longest edge is horizontal. Cut it in half down the middle vertically. Spoon a portion of the mixture on to each piece and roll up, tucking in the ends as you go, to make a spring roll shape. Do the same with the remaining mixture and halved filo sheets to make 8 rolls.

4 Put on a baking sheet lined with baking parchment and spray each with the cooking spray. Sprinkle with sesame seeds. Bake for 20 minutes until golden.

5 Stir together the sweet chilli sauce and 2 tablespoons water in a small bowl and put the soy sauce in a separate small bowl. Serve with the rolls and cucumber.

Cook's tip The filo pastry will keep in the packet, covered with clingfilm, in the fridge for up to three days. To use up the other two sheets, turn to page 72 for the Chicken, Squash and Spinach Filo Pie.

Try this This is a lovely lunch dish, but if you want to make it into more of a main meal, serve with 60 g (2 oz) dried rice per person, cooked according to packet instructions, and stir-fried broccoli, for an extra 6 **ProPoints** values per serving. You may also like to try it with the same quantities of shredded beef or pork instead for 5 **ProPoints** values and 6 **ProPoints** values, respectively.

Italian-style Chicken Livers

Chicken livers must be the bargain of the meat counter – they're incredible value, full of flavour and quick to cook too. Serve with 100 g (3½ oz) boiled potatoes per person for an additional 2 *ProPoints* values per serving, or 60 g (2 oz) dried tagliatelle, cooked according to packet instructions, and steamed vegetables, for an additional 6 *ProPoints* values per serving.

Serves 4
2 *ProPoints* values per serving
9 *ProPoints* values per recipe
35 minutes in total

calorie controlled cooking spray
1 onion, sliced
250 g (9 oz) chestnut mushrooms, sliced
400 g (14 oz) chicken livers, sliced
1 fresh thyme sprig, leaves only
1 tablespoon balsamic vinegar
1 tablespoon chopped fresh parsley
salt and freshly ground black pepper

1 Spray a non stick pan with the cooking spray and cook the onion for 5–8 minutes until golden around the edges. Add a splash of water if the onions start to stick.
2 Add the mushrooms and continue to cook for 3–5 minutes, tossing them around in the pan as they cook. After a couple of minutes, the mushrooms will start to release their juices.
3 Add the chicken livers and thyme leaves, season well and continue to cook for 6–8 minutes over a medium heat. Stir in the balsamic vinegar and parsley, and serve.

Chicken, Squash and Spinach Filo Pie

This recipe calls for just two sheets of filo pastry. You can use the other four sheets to make the Chicken Spring Rolls on page 71.

Serves 4
5 *ProPoints* values per serving
19 *ProPoints* values per recipe
40 minutes preparation, 20 minutes cooking

500 g (1 lb 2 oz) skinless boneless chicken breasts, cut into bite size pieces
1 garlic clove, sliced
1 fresh rosemary sprig, leaves only, chopped
calorie controlled cooking spray
1 onion, diced
2 celery sticks, diced
1 small butternut squash, peeled, de-seeded and cut into chunks
1 eating apple, peeled, cored and diced
400 ml (14 fl oz) hot chicken stock
50 g (1¾ oz) spinach, chopped finely
2 x 45 g sheets Jus-Rol filo pastry, each measuring 50 x 24 cm (20 x 9½ inches), defrosted if frozen
salt and freshly ground black pepper

1 Preheat the oven to Gas Mark 6/200°C/fan oven 180°C. Mix the chicken, garlic and rosemary in a bowl and set aside.
2 Spray a large lidded pan with the cooking spray and cook the onion, celery and squash, covered, for 10 minutes, until softened and golden.
3 Add the chicken and continue to cook for about 5 minutes until the chicken is just golden. Stir in the apple and stock. Season. Bring to the boil, then reduce to a simmer, cover and cook for 10 minutes until the chicken is cooked through. Stir in the spinach.
4 Spoon into a 2 litre (3½ pint) pie dish. Roughly scrunch up each filo pastry sheet and put on top of the dish, covering the filling. Spray with the cooking spray. Sprinkle with black pepper and bake in the oven for 20 minutes until the pastry is crisp, and then serve.

Stuffed Turkey Breast

Serve with 100 g (3½ oz) new potatoes and steamed green vegetables for an extra 2 **ProPoints** values per serving.

Serves 4
4 ProPoints values per serving
18 ProPoints values per recipe
30 minutes preparation, 40 minutes cooking

calorie controlled cooking spray
1 shallot, chopped finely
½ celery stick, chopped finely
1 garlic clove, crushed
1 fresh thyme sprig, leaves only
2 chopped fresh sage leaves
1 slice wholemeal calorie controlled bread, chopped finely
2 teaspoons apple chutney
1 tablespoon sultanas
350 ml (12 fl oz) hot chicken stock
500 g (1 lb 2 oz) skinless boneless turkey breast
3 slices prosciutto ham
150 ml (5 fl oz) boiling water
1 teaspoon cornflour
salt and freshly ground black pepper

1 Preheat the oven to Gas Mark 6/200°C/fan oven 180°C.
2 Spray a medium size pan with the cooking spray and cook the chopped shallot, celery and garlic with 1 tablespoon water for 5–8 minutes until softened and golden. Stir in the thyme and sage and cook for 1 minute. Tip into a bowl and cool a little. Stir in the bread, chutney and sultanas. Season well. Pour over 50 ml (2 fl oz) stock to moisten.
3 Put the turkey breast on a board and slice horizontally through the middle to create a pocket. Season, then stuff the filling into the pocket. Wrap the ham around the turkey and secure with a cocktail stick. Put in a flameproof roasting tin, pour the remaining stock into the tin and cover with foil. Roast for 40 minutes, removing the foil halfway through, until cooked all the way through. Pierce with a skewer to check the juices run clear.
4 Transfer the turkey to a warm plate, cover and keep warm. Put the roasting tin on the hob over a medium heat, add the boiling water to the tin and bring to the boil, stirring. Mix the cornflour with 1 tablespoon cold water. Add to the tin and simmer for 2–3 minutes until thickened and syrupy. Season to taste. Slice the turkey and serve with the gravy.

Zesty Pork with Spring Vegetable Stew

Slicing pork fillet into thin pieces gives this recipe its budget twist.

Serves 4
7 ProPoints values per serving
27 ProPoints values per recipe
30 minutes in total

400 g (14 oz) lean pork fillet, sliced thinly
juice and pared zest of ½ a lemon
1 fresh thyme sprig and 1 fresh rosemary sprig, leaves only, chopped
calorie controlled cooking spray
2 shallots, sliced
1 garlic clove, sliced
200 g (7 oz) carrots, peeled and sliced into chunks
400 g (14 oz) new potatoes, halved
600 ml (20 fl oz) hot chicken stock
200 g (7 oz) courgettes, sliced into chunks
100 g (3½ oz) green beans
4 tablespoons fresh or frozen peas
salt and freshly ground black pepper

1 Put the pork in a non metallic bowl and add the lemon zest and juice with the herbs. Set aside while you make the stew.
2 Spray a large casserole pan with the cooking spray and fry the shallots, garlic, carrots and new potatoes until just golden. Add the stock, season, and bring to a simmer. Cook for 15 minutes until the vegetables are just tender.
3 Spray a frying pan with the cooking spray, add the pork and marinade and cook over a high heat, turning, until golden.
4 Add the pork to the casserole pan, with any marinade, and tuck it down underneath the carrots and potatoes, using a wooden spoon. Then lay the courgettes and green beans on top. Cover and simmer again for 10 minutes, scattering the peas on top for the last 3 minutes.
5 Spoon into warmed bowls and serve.

Pork with Fennel and Rice

This delicious dish is flavoured with fennel and sweetened with raisins.

Serves 4
10 *ProPoints* values per serving
42 *ProPoints* values per recipe
15 minutes preparation,
     30 minutes cooking

calorie controlled cooking spray
1 onion, sliced
1 fennel bulb, chopped finely
1 garlic clove, chopped
15 g (½ oz) raisins
240 g (8½ oz) dried long grain brown rice
1.2 litres (2 pints) hot chicken stock
8 x 50 g (1¾ oz) pork escalopes
150 g (5½ oz) baby leaf spinach
salt and freshly ground black pepper
lemon wedges, to serve

1 Spray a large non stick frying pan with cooking spray and fry the onion over a low heat for around 15–20 minutes until softened. Add a drizzle of water every now and then to help it cook and caramelize without burning.

2 Spray a separate large lidded pan with the cooking spray and fry the fennel over a medium heat for 5 minutes until golden. Add the garlic and cook for 1 minute. Stir in the raisins, rice and chicken stock. Cover and simmer for 20–25 minutes.

3 Season the pork and add to the pan with the onions. Cook for 3–4 minutes on each side until golden and cooked through.

4 Just before the rice has finished cooking, add the spinach and let it wilt. Spoon the rice on to plates with the pork, the caramelized onions and lemon wedges.

Try this For an even cheaper option, you could use the same amount of turkey fillets instead of pork escalopes for 9 ***ProPoints*** values per serving.

Mediterranean Marrow

Stuffing this large late-summer vegetable with a tasty mixture of meat and vegetables is a canny way of filling your plate with lots of goodness.

Serves 4

3 *ProPoints* values per serving
11 *ProPoints* values per recipe
10 minutes preparation, 50 minutes cooking

25 g (1 oz) slice brown bread
250 g (9 oz) turkey mince
4 spring onions, chopped roughly
1 red pepper, de-seeded and diced
¼ teaspoon ground cinnamon
½ teaspoon ground coriander
a pinch of chilli flakes
1 fresh thyme sprig, leaves only
1 marrow
300 ml (10 fl oz) hot chicken stock
25 g (1 oz) Parmesan cheese, freshly grated
salt and freshly ground black pepper

1 Preheat the oven to Gas Mark 5/190°C/fan oven 170°C. Whizz the bread in a food processor or with a hand blender to make breadcrumbs. Remove a third of it, and reserve in a small bowl.
2 Put the turkey mince and spring onions in the food processor or hand blender with the remaining breadcrumbs and whizz to mix the ingredients together thoroughly. Tip into a bowl and add the red pepper, cinnamon, coriander, chilli flakes and thyme. Season and mix everything together.
3 Halve the marrow lengthways and scoop out the seeds. Fill each half with half of the meat mixture. Put in a roasting tin lined with foil. Pour the stock slowly over, then seal the foil edges to make a parcel. Cook in the oven for 40 minutes.
4 Uncover the parcel and sprinkle over the remaining breadcrumbs, followed by the Parmesan. Return to the oven to allow the breadcrumbs to brown and the cheese to melt, then slice each marrow half in two and serve immediately.

American-style Beans

Preparing and cooking dried beans takes a little more time and effort, but they are a fraction of the cost of tinned beans. If you want to use canned beans, use 2 x 400 g cans, drained and rinsed, for the same ***ProPoints*** values per serving and replace the cooking liquid in step 4 with the same amount of boiling water.

Serves 4

5 *ProPoints* values per serving
21 *ProPoints* values per recipe
20 minutes preparation + overnight soaking,
   1 hour 15 minutes cooking

200 g (7 oz) dried cannellini beans
1 onion, sliced
1 bay leaf
calorie controlled cooking spray
1 garlic clove, crushed
350 g (12 oz) passata with basil
a good dash or two of Worcestershire sauce
2 teaspoons tomato ketchup
1 teaspoon dark brown muscovado sugar
a small handful of chopped fresh parsley
4 rashers back bacon, all visible fat removed
150 g (5½ oz) baby leaf spinach, washed
4 medium slices wholemeal bread

1 Soak the cannellini beans in cold water overnight.
2 The next day, drain the beans and put in a medium lidded pan with the onion and bay leaf. Cover with cold water and then cover the pan. Bring to the boil and then turn the heat down to low and simmer for 45 minutes to 1 hour until the beans are tender.
3 Spray a medium pan with the cooking spray and cook the garlic for 1 minute.
4 Drain the beans and onion, reserving 200 ml (7 fl oz) of the cooking liquid. Add the beans to the pan with the passata, Worcestershire sauce, tomato ketchup and sugar. Bring to the boil and then reduce the heat and simmer for 15 minutes. Discard the bay leaf. Stir in the parsley.
5 Preheat the grill to medium and cook the bacon.
6 Put the spinach in a pan, cover and heat for 1–2 minutes until just wilted (or simply put on the toast and let the beans wilt it). Toast the bread then put the slices on the four plates. Divide the spinach among them, then top with the beans and bacon.

Saucy Mediterranean Stew

This one-pot dish combines pork tenderloin and red lentils for a delicious supper.

Serves 4

9 *ProPoints* values per serving
37 *ProPoints* values per recipe
30 minutes preparation, 20 minutes cooking

calorie controlled cooking spray
1 small onion, chopped
2 celery sticks, chopped
1 red pepper, de-seeded and chopped
400 g (14 oz) lean pork fillet, cut into small pieces
1 teaspoon paprika
¼ teaspoon chilli flakes
400 g can chopped tomatoes
75 g (2¾ oz) dried red lentils, rinsed
150 g (5½ oz) dried long grain rice
600 ml (20 fl oz) hot chicken stock
1–2 tablespoons chopped fresh parsley
salt and freshly ground black pepper

1 Spray a large lidded pan with the cooking spray and cook the onion over a medium heat with a drizzle of water for 5–10 minutes until just golden. Add the celery and pepper and continue to cook for 4–5 minutes.
2 Add the pork, paprika and chilli flakes to the pan, season, and cook for 2–3 minutes. Stir in the chopped tomatoes, lentils, rice and stock, then cover and cook for 20 minutes until the rice is cooked.
3 Stir in the parsley and serve.

Mexican Salad with Cheesy Tortillas

Tortillas are toasted to become crisps and keep the *ProPoints* values low.

Serves 4

8 *ProPoints* values per serving
34 *ProPoints* values per recipe
25 minutes in total

1 red pepper, de-seeded and cut into quarters
400 g can black eyed beans in water, drained and rinsed
3 tomatoes, chopped
3 spring onions, sliced
2 teaspoons red wine vinegar
2 x 60 g (2 oz) wholemeal tortillas
50 g (1¾ oz) half fat Cheddar cheese, grated
2 Little Gem lettuces, shredded
100 g (3½ oz) skinless cooked chicken breast, shredded
1 avocado, chopped
salt and freshly ground black pepper

1 Preheat the grill to medium high. Put the pepper quarters skin-side up on a non stick baking sheet and grill until blackened. Put in a bowl, cover with a plate and set aside for 10 minutes to loosen the skin. Peel off the skin and discard, then chop the peppers.
2 Put the black eyed beans in a bowl, stir in the tomatoes, spring onions, red pepper and vinegar. Season and stir everything together.
3 Lightly toast the tortillas under the grill on one side. Turn over and scatter the cheese on top. Grill until bubbling and golden.
4 Put the lettuce in a bowl, spoon the beans over the top, followed by the chicken and the avocado. Cut the toasted tortillas into wedges and serve alongside.

This version of a popular fast food favourite is fun to eat and great for sharing.

Turkey Stew with Lentils and Spinach

If you fancy a stew, turkey is a great quick-cook meat. Here it's teamed with green lentils and spinach for a wholesome supper. Serve with 60 g (2 oz) dried brown rice per person, cooked according to packet instructions, for an extra 6 **ProPoints** values per serving.

Serves 4
5 ProPoints values per serving
19 ProPoints values per recipe
20 minutes preparation, 45 minutes cooking

calorie controlled cooking spray
1 onion, chopped finely
1 carrot, peeled and chopped finely
1 celery stick, chopped finely
400 g (14 oz) skinless boneless turkey breast,
   cut into bite size pieces
850 ml (1½ pints) of chicken stock
1 fresh rosemary sprig
100 g (3½ oz) puy or green lentils
100 g (3½ oz) baby leaf spinach
2 tablespoons chopped fresh parsley
salt and freshly ground black pepper

1 Heat a lidded casserole dish and spray with the cooking spray. Gently cook the chopped onion, carrot and celery, covered, for 10–15 minutes until starting to turn golden.
2 Add the turkey to the pan, season, and cook to brown all over. Pour over the stock, add the rosemary sprig and cover. Turn the heat down to low and cook for 20 minutes.
3 Meanwhile, put the lentils in a lidded saucepan and cover with cold water. Bring to the boil. Turn the heat down to low and simmer for about 15 minutes until just al dente. Drain well, then stir into the turkey with the spinach and parsley and serve.

Lamb and Chick Pea Burgers

Here's a twist on traditional burgers. They're made with lamb mince, filling chick peas, sweet apricots and a pinch of spice. These are delicious with chunky sweet potato wedges.

Serves 4
10 ProPoints values per serving
41 ProPoints values per recipe
20 minutes preparation, 40 minutes cooking

550 g (1 lb 3 oz) sweet potatoes, unpeeled,
   cut into thin wedges
calorie controlled cooking spray
250 g (9 oz) lean lamb mince
400 g can chick peas in water,
   drained and rinsed
4 spring onions, chopped roughly
6 ready-to-eat dried apricots
a pinch of dried chilli flakes
4 large beef tomatoes, halved
4 large leaves Little Gem lettuce
4 tablespoons virtually fat free plain yogurt
4 teaspoons apple chutney or vegetable pickle
salt and freshly ground black pepper

1 Preheat the oven to Gas Mark 6/200°C/fan oven 180°C. Put the sweet potatoes on a baking sheet, spray with the cooking spray, season generously and roast for 40 minutes, turning occasionally.
2 Put the lamb in a food processor with the chick peas, spring onions, apricots and chilli flakes. Pulse to chop all the ingredients and to blend the mixture together – the mixture should still have a little bit of texture.
3 Tip into a bowl and, using wet hands, shape the mixture into four burgers. Heat a medium frying pan to a high heat, spray with the cooking spray and then fry the burgers until golden on each side. Put on another baking sheet with the halved tomatoes and cook in the oven under the potato wedges for 25–30 minutes.
4 Put the tomato halves on each plate and top one half with a burger. Add a leaf of Little Gem lettuce topped with yogurt and chutney. Serve with the potato wedges.

Calzone

This Italian version of a pasty is made with dough instead of pastry. They are delicious served with a quick-to-make tomato sauce.

Serves 2

9 ProPoints values per serving
19 ProPoints values per recipe
20 minutes preparation + 40 minutes rising, 20 minutes cooking

100 g (3½ oz) strong plain or wholemeal bread flour, plus extra for dusting
¼ teaspoon instant dried yeast (see Cook's tip)
¼ teaspoon salt
2 x 35 g (1¼ oz) slices lean smoked ham, all visible fat removed
125 g (4½ oz) light mozzarella cheese, sliced
50 g (1¾ oz) spinach
200 g (7 oz) passata with basil
1 garlic clove, sliced
1 teaspoon balsamic vinegar
salt and freshly ground black pepper

1 Preheat the oven to Gas Mark 8/230°C/fan oven 210°C. Put a non stick baking sheet in the oven to preheat.

2 Put the flour in a bowl and stir in the yeast and salt. Make a well in the middle, pour in 75–100 ml (3–3½ fl oz) lukewarm water and stir until the mixture comes together. Dust a board lightly with flour and then knead the dough on the board for about 5 minutes until soft and sticky. Put in a bowl, cover with clingfilm, and set aside to rise for 40 minutes.

3 Put the dough on a floured board and cut in half. Roll each half out to make two 19 cm (7½ inch) circles.

4 Place a slice of ham on one half of each circle, then top each with half the sliced mozzarella, then a few leaves of spinach. Season well. Fold over the other half of each one and seal by wrapping the edge of the dough over and pinching to secure. Slide on to the hot baking sheet and bake for 15–20 minutes until the dough is cooked and the calzone sounds hollow when you tap it on the top.

5 A few minutes before the calzone comes out of the oven, put the passata in a small pan with the garlic and balsamic vinegar. Bring to a simmer to heat through.

6 Put each calzone on a plate, spoon over the passata and serve immediately.

Cook's tips Any remaining passata can be kept in the fridge for 3 days or frozen for up to three months in a freezable lidded container.

You don't need a lot of yeast to make the calzone dough rise and any leftover yeast from the packet will keep well in the cupboard for weeks. You could also use it in any of the other bread recipes in this book such as the Seeded Rolls on page 105 or the Courgette Tear-and-Share Loaf on page 102.

Beef and Vegetable Stew

Serves 4

8 *ProPoints* values per serving
32 *ProPoints* values per recipe
30 minutes preparation, 2 hours 10 minutes cooking

calorie controlled cooking spray
450 g (1 lb) casserole or stewing beef, visible fat removed
1 tablespoon plain flour
1 onion, chopped
2 celery sticks, chopped
2 carrots (225 g/8 oz), peeled and chopped
1 swede (450 g/1 lb), peeled and chopped
2 small turnips, peeled and chopped
850 ml (1½ pints) hot beef stock
150 g (5½ oz) button mushrooms
2 fresh rosemary stalks
70 g (2½ oz) baguette, cut into four thick slices
1 garlic clove, halved
2 tablespoons finely chopped fresh parsley
salt and freshly ground black pepper

1 Preheat the oven to Gas Mark 3/160°C/fan oven 140°C.
2 Heat a large, lidded, flame and ovenproof casserole dish to a medium high heat, then spray with the cooking spray. Brown the beef, remove from the pan and set aside.
3 Add all the vegetables, except the mushrooms to the pan, sprinkle over the flour and mix into the vegetables. Reduce the heat, cover and cook for 3–5 minutes.
4 Slowly stir in the stock, then return the meat to the pan. Season, cover, and bring to the boil on the hob then transfer to the oven for 2 hours until the meat is tender. After 1½ hours, stir in the mushrooms and rosemary and cook for a further 30 minutes.
5 When the stew is cooked, spray one side of each of the baguette slices with cooking spray and rub with garlic. Arrange the bread around the edge of the casserole, then sprinkle over the parsley. Return the casserole to the oven, uncovered, for 10 minutes, remove the rosemary stalks and then serve.

Try this Add 150 g (5½ oz) beef kidney, chopped, for 9 ***ProPoints*** values per serving. Simply brown it in the pan after the beef in step 2 and return with the meat to the pan in step 4.

Chilli Beef Ramen

A warming bowl of noodles, vegetables and beef that will hit the spot for lunch or dinner anytime.

Serves 4

8 *ProPoints* values per serving
32 *ProPoints* values per recipe
30 minutes in total

4 cm (1½ inches) fresh root ginger, sliced
2 garlic cloves, crushed
1–2 red or green chillies (to taste), de-seeded and chopped finely
250 g (9 oz) frying steak
1.2 litres (2 pints) hot beef stock
calorie controlled cooking spray
200 g (7 oz) dried fine egg noodles
1 carrot, peeled and sliced into small batons
½ bag beansprouts
¼ Chinese leaf lettuce, shredded finely
½ red pepper, de-seeded and sliced finely
a small handful of fresh coriander leaves
salt and freshly ground black pepper

1 Mix the ginger, garlic and chilli together in a bowl to make a paste to marinate the steak. Put the steak in a non metallic dish and spoon over two-thirds of the chilli mixture. Toss to coat.
2 Pour the stock into a medium lidded saucepan and add the remaining ginger, garlic and chilli mixture to the pan. Cover the pan, bring to the boil, then reduce the heat and simmer for 5 minutes to flavour the stock.
3 Season the beef then spray a medium non stick frying pan with the cooking spray, add the beef and fry over a high heat for 1–2 minutes on each side until browned, but still pink in the middle. Remove the beef and slice thinly. Add any juices and bits of chilli mixture still in the frying pan to the pan of stock.
4 Add the noodles and carrots to the pan with the stock and cook for 2–3 minutes. Stir in the beansprouts, cabbage and the pepper and simmer for 1–2 minutes more. Ladle into warm bowls, then place the beef and coriander leaves on top and serve.

Delicately flavoured with chilli, garlic and ginger, this beef soup is sure to become a favourite.

Baked Sweet Potatoes with Spicy Mince and Beans

The natural sweetness of sweet potatoes combines perfectly with a spicy beef filling.

Serves 4
10 *ProPoints* values per serving
39 *ProPoints* values per recipe
15 minutes preparation,
    40 minutes cooking

4 x 150 g (5½ oz) sweet potatoes
calorie controlled cooking spray
1 small onion, diced
300 g (10½ oz) extra lean beef mince
300 ml (10 fl oz) hot beef stock
a pinch of chilli flakes
1 tablespoon tomato purée
400 g can pinto beans in water, drained and
    rinsed (see Cook's tip)
4 spring onions, sliced (optional)
4 teaspoons virtually fat free plain yogurt

1 Preheat the oven to Gas Mark 6/200°C/fan oven 180°C. Put the sweet potatoes on a baking sheet, prick all over and then bake in the oven for 30–40 minutes until tender.
2 Heat a large saucepan over a medium heat and spray with the cooking spray. Cook the onion for 5 minutes until golden, then add the mince and brown all over, breaking it up with the back of a spoon.
3 Stir in the beef stock, chilli flakes, tomato purée and beans and simmer for 40 minutes.
4 Put the sweet potatoes on individual plates. Split them open and spoon in the mince mixture. Top with the spring onions, if using, and the yogurt, then serve.

Cook's tip Instead of pinto beans, you could use any can of beans of the same weight. Just remember to adjust the ***ProPoints*** values.

Steak with Black Beans and Corn Salsa

Make frying steak go further by slicing it thinly and serving it with saucy black beans and a refreshing salsa.

Serves 2
10 ProPoints values per serving
20 ProPoints values per recipe
30 minutes in total

400 g can black beans in water, *drained and rinsed*
150 ml (5 fl oz) hot chicken stock
calorie controlled cooking spray
250 g (9 oz) frying steak
120 g (4½ oz) frozen sweetcorn, *thawed*
2 tablespoons ready-made tomato salsa
1 tablespoon chopped fresh coriander
salt and freshly ground black pepper
40 g (1½ oz) rocket, *to garnish*
½ a lime, cut in half, to serve

1 Put the beans in a small saucepan with the stock and heat through gently.
2 Heat a non stick frying pan over a medium heat and spray with the cooking spray. Season the steak and fry for 2–3 minutes on each side. Put on a board to rest for a few minutes.
3 Mix together the sweetcorn, salsa and coriander. Divide the beans between two bowls, then slice the steak and put on top. Spoon over the sweetcorn salsa, garnish with rocket and serve with the lime.

Hot Beef Pockets

Warm pitta breads, pan-fried steak and a handful of colourful vegetables cooked in a sticky sweet sauce make this an ideal quick lunch or supper dish.

Serves 4
8 ProPoints values per serving
31 ProPoints values per recipe
20 minutes in total

calorie controlled cooking spray
350 g (12 oz) frying steak
1 small red pepper, *de-seeded and sliced*
1 small courgette, *cut into batons*
a pinch of dried chilli flakes
1 tablespoon red wine vinegar
1 tablespoon clear honey
4 medium pitta breads
4 small tomatoes, *sliced*
1 Little Gem lettuce, *shredded*
salt and freshly ground black pepper

1 Heat a medium frying pan until hot and spray with the cooking spray. Season the steak and fry on each side for 2–3 minutes. Set aside to rest.
2 Add the sliced peppers and courgettes to the pan with the chilli flakes and spray again with the cooking spray. Cook for 5 minutes. Mix the vinegar, honey and 2 tablespoons of water and add to the pan. Stir everything together.
3 Warm the pitta breads and slice one edge of each to open. Slice the steak then divide equally among the pittas with the vegetables, tomatoes and lettuce. Serve at once.

Beef and Mushroom Stroganoff

This Russian classic is given a twist by adding some tasty green beans.

Serves 4
10 *ProPoints* values per serving
40 *ProPoints* values per recipe
30 minutes in total

225 g (8 oz) dried tagliatelle or papardelle
300 g (10½ oz) frying steak, sliced into
   1 cm (½ inch) pieces
1 teaspoon cornflour
1 teaspoon paprika
calorie controlled cooking spray
2 shallots, sliced
250 g (9 oz) mushrooms, sliced
150 g (5½ oz) green beans, halved
   lengthways
2 tablespoons half fat crème fraîche
salt and freshly ground black pepper

1 Bring a large pan of water to the boil and cook the pasta according to the packet instructions.

2 Meanwhile, toss the steak in the cornflour and paprika, then season. Spray a medium lidded saucepan with the cooking spray and add the shallots and mushrooms and cover, cooking until just golden. Tip on to a plate.

3 Continue to heat the pan until medium hot and add the steak. Cook quickly in the heat of the pan until browned for 3–5 minutes, then return the shallot mixture to the pan. Add the green beans and 3 tablespoons water and cook for a few minutes more until tender.

4 Stir in the crème fraîche. Cover again and cook for 2 minutes longer.

5 Drain the pasta well then divide among four plates. Spoon over the sauce and serve.

Bakes & Puddings

Lemon Yogurt Ice with Hot Blueberries

This rich and creamy pudding is perfect for serving a crowd. It will also keep well, wrapped in clingfilm, in the freezer for up to one month.

Serves 6
2 ProPoints values per serving
16 ProPoints values per recipe
15 minutes in total + freezing
V ✳

500 g pot virtually fat free plain yogurt
2 teaspoons finely grated lemon zest
75 g (2¾ oz) golden caster sugar, plus
    1 teaspoon extra
350 g (12 oz) frozen blueberries

1 Stir together the yogurt, lemon zest and 75 g (2¾ oz) of the caster sugar and put in a shallow freezerproof container. Seal and freeze for about 1 hour. Remove from the freezer and stir with a fork to break down the ice crystals. Return to the freezer and repeat the process twice more.

2 Spray or sprinkle a 450 g (1 lb) loaf tin with water and then line it with clingfilm, spoon the mixture into the tin and freeze until completely solid.

3 When ready to serve, put the blueberries and 1 teaspoon of sugar in a pan with 1 tablespoon water and heat gently to thaw the fruit until it is heated through and the juices run. Unwrap the yogurt ice, then cut into slices and serve with a spoonful of the blueberries and syrup over the top.

Cook's tip If you can't find frozen blueberries, use the same quantity of frozen mixed berries for the same **ProPoints** values.

Orange Bramley Crumble

The topping is made by rubbing together just a little bit of flour with oats and a few flaked almonds for a granola-style topping. Serve with 60 g (2 oz) virtually fat free plain yogurt per person for an extra 1 *ProPoints* value per serving or 60 g (2 oz) low fat ice cream per person for an extra 2 *ProPoints* values per serving.

Serves 4
5 *ProPoints* values per serving
19 *ProPoints* values per recipe
15 minutes preparation, 30 minutes cooking
V

3 Bramley apples (about 750 g/1 lb 10 oz), peeled, cored
   and chopped very small
40 g (1½ oz) light muscovado sugar
zest and juice of ½ an orange
a good pinch of cinnamon
50 g (1¾ oz) plain flour
50 g (1¾ oz) porridge oats
a pinch of salt
20 g (¾ oz) low fat spread
15 g (½ oz) flaked almonds

1 Preheat the oven to Gas Mark 4/180°C/fan oven 160°C. Toss the apple in a bowl with half of the sugar, the orange zest and juice and the cinnamon. Spoon into a 20 cm (8 inch) square ovenproof dish.
2 Put the flour, oats and salt in a mixing bowl and add the low fat spread. Rub it in with your fingertips until the mixture resembles breadcrumbs, then stir in the almonds and the rest of the sugar.
3 Sprinkle the topping evenly over the apple mixture. Bake for 30 minutes until the topping is crisp and golden and the apple is tender.

Meringue and Ice Cream Peaches

Peaches are filled with ice cream and mallowy meringue to create a simple yet stunning dessert.

Serves 4
3 *ProPoints* values per serving
11 *ProPoints* values per recipe
10 minutes in total
V

411 g can peach halves in natural juice, drained
1 egg white
50 g (1¾ oz) golden caster sugar
1 tablespoon ground almonds
60 g (2 oz) low fat vanilla ice cream

1 Line a non stick baking sheet with foil. Cut a slim slice off the rounded side of each peach and sit it on the foil-lined baking sheet.
2 Preheat the grill to its highest setting.
3 Whisk the egg white using an electric hand whisk in a clean grease-free bowl until just stiff – around 2 minutes. Add the sugar, a little at a time, and continue to whisk until the meringue is very stiff and glossy. Gently fold in half of the ground almonds, using a metal spoon.
4 Divide the ice cream between the peach hollows. Spoon over the meringue, sprinkle with the remaining almonds and grill for 1–2 minutes until golden. Serve immediately.

Baked Apples

A twist on a classic, using dried apricots and stem ginger. Serve with 60 g (2 oz) virtually fat free plain yogurt per person for an extra 1 **ProPoints** value per serving or 60 g (2 oz) low fat ice cream per person for an extra 2 **ProPoints** values per serving.

Serves 4
2 ProPoints values per serving
7 ProPoints values per recipe
15 minutes preparation, 55 minutes cooking
V

4 Bramley apples
6 dried apricots, chopped
2 balls preserved stem ginger in syrup,
   drained and chopped
½ teaspoon ground mixed spice
zest and juice of an orange
2 teaspoons light soft brown sugar
½ a kettleful of boiling water

1 Preheat the oven to Gas Mark 6/200°C/fan oven 180°C.
2 Core the apples, then score each using a sharp knife around the middle. Put in an ovenproof dish. Mix together the apricots, stem ginger, mixed spice, orange zest and juice, then spoon equally among the cored apples. Sprinkle over the sugar. Pour 100 ml (3½ fl oz) boiling water into the bottom of the dish.
3 Cover with foil and cook for 55 minutes, removing the foil for the last 10 minutes.

Cook's tip You could use windfall cooking apples from the garden if you have them.

Hot Berry Roll Ups

Frozen fruits are a brilliant freezer standby for making puddings. Here they're wrapped in an envelope of filo pastry and sprinkled with sugar for a delectable crisp crust, then drizzled with some warm custard.

Serves 4
3 ProPoints values per serving
11 ProPoints values per recipe
15 minutes preparation, 20 minutes cooking
V

2 x 45 g Jus-Rol filo pastry sheets, each measuring 50 x 24 cm
   (20 x 9½ inches), defrosted if frozen
400 g (14 oz) frozen fruits
1 teaspoon orange zest
1 tablespoon caster sugar
calorie controlled cooking spray

For the custard
1 tablespoon custard powder
75 ml (3 fl oz) skimmed milk
1 teaspoon sugar

1 Preheat the oven to Gas Mark 6/200°C/fan oven 180°C.
2 Put a sheet of filo on a board, with the longest side horizontal. Cut in half to form two squares.
3 Mix together three quarters of the frozen fruits with the orange zest and ½ tablespoon sugar. Put a quarter on to the bottom of one square, fold in the sides, then roll up from the bottom. Spray a baking sheet with cooking spray, put the pastry on the baking sheet and spray again with the cooking spray. Repeat to make four rolled up parcels.
4 Sprinkle over the remaining sugar and bake for 15–20 minutes until golden and crisp. Warm the remaining fruit in a small pan to serve with the roll ups.
5 Make up the custard powder according to packet instructions, mixing it with the milk, 75 ml (3 fl oz) water and the sugar. Serve each roll up with the warm fruits and 2 tablespoons of warm custard.

Ginger Biscuits

These spicy biscuits, studded with chunks of stem ginger, have a delicious chewy texture and are perfect with a cup of tea.

Makes 18
2 *ProPoints* value per serving
35 *ProPoints* values per recipe
15 minutes preparation, 15 minutes cooking
V ✳

75 g (2¾ oz) light muscovado sugar
40 g (1½ oz) low fat spread
175 g (6 oz) self-raising flour
½ level teaspoon bicarbonate of soda
1 level teaspoon ground ginger
3 balls preserved stem ginger in syrup, drained and chopped
1 tablespoon ginger syrup from the jar
1 egg, beaten

1 Preheat the oven to Gas Mark 4/180ºC/fan oven 160ºC. Line two baking sheets with baking parchment.
2 Cream the sugar and low fat spread together in a large bowl using a wooden spoon. Reserving 1 teaspoon of flour for rolling in step 4, sift over the flour, bicarbonate of soda and ginger, then add the stem ginger, ginger syrup and beaten egg.
3 Mix with the wooden spoon until the mixture looks like a crumbly dough. Continue to work the mixture together until it looks pliable, then knead with your hands to bring it all together.
4 Take a piece of the mixture, between the size of a walnut and a fresh apricot, and roll roughly into a ball. Put on the parchment. Repeat to make 18 pieces. If the mixture feels sticky, use some of the reserved flour to dust over.
5 Press the back of a fork into the reserved flour, then use to press down and flatten the balls, flouring the fork every now and then. Bake in the oven for 15 minutes. Halfway through cooking, press the biscuits down again with the fork.
6 Transfer to a wire rack to cool. They may feel soft when you slide them on to the rack but they'll firm up on cooling. Store in an airtight tin for up to five days.

Cook's tip Stem ginger in syrup keeps well in a cool dark place or in the fridge. Grate or chop a ball and stir into the fruit base of a crumble with a drizzle of the syrup or use as part of a filling for Baked Apples on page 98.

Chocolate Sponge

This feather-light chocolate sponge makes the perfect after-dinner treat.

Serves 10
4 *ProPoints* values per serving
38 *ProPoints* values per recipe
20 minutes preparation, 30 minutes cooking
V ✳

calorie controlled cooking spray
3 eggs
125 g (4½ oz) golden caster sugar
125 g (4½ oz) self-raising flour
50 g (1¾ oz) cocoa
1 teaspoon vanilla extract
50 g (1¾ oz) Weight Watchers Reduced Sugar Apricot Jam
10 g (¼ oz) at least 70% cocoa solids dark chocolate

1 Preheat the oven to Gas Mark 4/180°C/fan oven 160°C. Spray a 20 cm (8 inch) round cake tin with the cooking spray and line the base and sides with baking parchment.
2 Put the eggs and sugar in a large bowl and whisk with an electric hand whisk on full speed for 5 minutes until the mixture has doubled in size and is foamy. The whisks should leave a ribbon-like trail when lifted up, and at this stage the top of the mixture will be covered in small bubbles.
3 Sift over the flour and cocoa and drizzle over the vanilla. Gently fold together with a metal spoon and then pour into the prepared cake tin. Bake for 20–30 minutes until the mixture is set and the top springs back when pressed lightly on top.
4 Turn out the cake on to a cooling rack and allow to cool. Remove the parchment and use a serrated bread knife to cut horizontally through the cake. Spread the base with the apricot jam. Replace the top and put on a plate. Grate over the chocolate and serve.

Serving suggestion Serve the cake with some raspberries, blueberries and sliced strawberries, and 60 g (2 oz) low fat ice cream per person, for an extra 2 ***ProPoints*** values per serving.

Cook's tip Wrap the sponge in clingfilm and freeze for up to 1 month.

Courgette Tear-and-Share Loaf

Using grated courgette gives this bread a really moist texture – it's delicious lightly toasted.

Serves 10

3 *ProPoints* values per serving

33 *ProPoints* values per recipe

30 minutes preparation + rising and
   proving time, 35 minutes cooking

V ✳

200 g (7 oz) wholemeal strong bread flour

100 g (3½ oz) plain white flour, plus
   1 tablespoon extra, to dust

1 teaspoon instant dried yeast

125 g (4½ oz) courgette, grated coarsely

1 tablespoon sunflower seeds

½ teaspoon salt

1 Line a baking sheet with foil or baking parchment.

2 Sift the flours into a bowl and stir in the yeast, grated courgette, sunflower seeds and salt. Make a well in the centre and pour in 150–175 ml (5–6 fl oz) lukewarm water. Mix with a knife to bring all the ingredients together to make a rough dough, then tip on to a floured board and knead for around 5 minutes until soft and sticky. Return to the bowl, cover and leave to rise for 30 minutes.

3 Dust a board with the reserved flour. Tip the dough on to it and, kneading it very lightly with your hands, roughly shape into a uniform oblong loaf shape, measuring 25 x 8 cm (10 x 3¼ inches). Put on the prepared baking sheet and mark into slices: use a bread knife to slice the loaf at about 2.5 cm (1 inch) intervals, about three quarters of the way down through the loaf to make 10 slices, but still keeping the loaf in one piece. Set aside for 30 minutes until the dough springs back when pushed gently with a finger. Preheat the oven to Gas Mark 6/200°C/fan oven 180°C.

4 Bake for around 30–35 minutes until risen and golden and the loaf sounds hollow when tapped on the base.

Cook's tip Wrap the loaf well in clingfilm and freeze for up to 1 month. Thaw overnight at a cool room temperature and enjoy.

Savoury Rosemary Oatcakes

Serves 8

2 ProPoints values per serving (3 oatcakes)

16 ProPoints values per recipe

15 minutes preparation, 14 minutes cooking

V

50 g (1¾ oz) plain flour, plus extra for dusting

50 g (1¾ oz) rolled oats

40 g (1½ oz) reduced fat spread

1 fresh rosemary sprig, leaves chopped finely

15 g (½ oz) Parmesan cheese, grated finely

salt and freshly ground black pepper

1 Preheat the oven to Gas Mark 4/180°C/fan oven 160°C.

2 Put the flour, oats and reduced fat spread in a bowl with the chopped rosemary. Season well. Rub in the fat until the mixture looks like breadcrumbs then add the cheese and 3 tablespoons of cold water.

3 Bring the mixture together into a ball and put on a sheet of clingfilm. Put another sheet of clingfilm on top and roll the mixture out thinly, about 3 mm (¹/₈ inch) thick.

4 Stamp out 24 rounds using a 5 cm (2 inch) cutter, re-rolling the dough between the clingfilm as necessary. Prick with a fork.

5 Place on a non stick baking sheet and bake for 7 minutes. Turn the rounds over and cook for a further 7 minutes. Cool on a wire rack and store in an airtight container for up to 1 week.

Cook's tip Rolling the dough in clingfilm makes it easier to get the mixture really thin and saves a messy work surface.

Try this Swap the rosemary for a sprig of fresh thyme or fresh oregano.

Golden Tea Loaf

You must try this gorgeous fruit-rich cake. Dried apricots and sultanas soaked in tea mixed with a kick of sweet stem ginger make it lovely and moist.

Makes 18 slices

4 ProPoints values per serving

68 ProPoints values per recipe

15 minutes preparation + overnight soaking, 1 hour cooking

V ✳

75 g (2¾ oz) dried apricots, chopped

125 g (4½ oz) sultanas

150 ml (5 fl oz) freshly made, hot Earl Grey tea

calorie controlled cooking spray

150 g (5½ oz) self-raising flour, plus extra to dust

50 g (1¾ oz) light muscovado sugar

2 balls stem ginger in syrup, drained and chopped

2 eggs, beaten

1 teaspoon ground mixed spice

1 Put the apricots and sultanas in a bowl and pour the tea over. Set aside to soak for at least 8 hours.

2 Preheat the oven to Gas Mark 5/190°C/fan oven 170°C. Spray a 450 g (1 lb) loaf tin with the cooking spray and dust with flour.

3 Put the soaked fruit into a large bowl, add the flour, sugar, stem ginger, eggs and mixed spice. Beat everything together with a wooden spoon until well mixed. Spoon into the tin and bake for 1 hour. Cool in the tin for 1 hour, then remove and cool completely on a wire rack before slicing.

Cook's tip To freeze, wrap in clingfilm and freeze either whole or in slices for up to 1 month.

Seeded Rolls

A sprinkling of seeds and herbs make these special. Serve with the Summer Greens Soup on page 10.

Makes 12 rolls
3 *ProPoints* values per serving
38 *ProPoints* values per recipe
15 minutes preparation + rising and proving
    time, 15 minutes cooking
V ✳

175 g (6 oz) strong wholemeal bread flour, plus
    1 teaspoon for kneading
175 g (6 oz) strong granary bread flour
1½ teaspoons instant dried yeast
1 tablespoon seeds, such as sesame seeds,
    poppy seeds or sunflower seeds
1 teaspoon dried chives
½ teaspoon salt
1 teaspoon plain flour, for kneading

1 Line a baking sheet with baking parchment
2 Sift the flours into a bowl, adding any bits left behind in the sieve to the bowl, and stir in the yeast, seeds, dried chives and salt. Make a well in the centre and pour in 200 ml (7 fl oz) lukewarm water. Mix with a knife to make a rough dough, then tip on to a lightly floured board and knead until soft and sticky. Return to the bowl, cover and leave to rise for 30 minutes.
3 Tip the dough on to a lightly floured board and divide into 12 small pieces. Roll each into a round and put on the prepared baking sheet then set aside for 30 minutes until the dough springs back when pushed gently with a finger. Preheat the oven to Gas Mark 6/200°C/fan oven 180°C.
4 Bake for 15 minutes until risen and golden and the rolls sound hollow when tapped on the base.

Cook's tip Wrap in clingfilm and freeze for up to 1 month.

Savoury Red Pepper Muffins

These bite size muffins have a deliciously nutty flavour and texture and are best served warm.

Makes 24
1 *ProPoints* value per serving
29 *ProPoints* values per recipe
20 minutes preparation,
    20 minutes cooking
V ✳

calorie controlled cooking spray
1 small onion, chopped finely
1 red pepper, de-seeded and diced
2–3 fresh thyme sprigs, leaves only, chopped,
    or a pinch of dried
175 g (6 oz) wholemeal flour
75 g (2¾ oz) plain flour
1 teaspoon baking powder
200 g (7 oz) 0% fat Greek yogurt
2 eggs
salt and freshly ground black pepper

1 Preheat the oven to Gas Mark 6/200°C/fan oven 180°C. Spray the holes of two 12-hole muffin tins (or simply use one tin and cook in two batches) with the cooking spray.
2 Spray a non stick frying pan with the cooking spray and cook the onion and pepper in the pan over a medium heat for 5–10 minutes until golden and softened. Season well. Stir the thyme leaves into the pan and cook for 1 minute. Set aside to cool.
3 Sift both types of flour and the baking powder into a bowl. Add the cooled cooked vegetables and toss to mix together. Beat the yogurt, eggs and 3 tablespoons of water together in a separate bowl and season well. Make a well in the centre of the flour mixture and pour in the yogurt mixture. Roughly mix everything together with a large metal spoon until just combined – it's fine if there are a few floury bits. Spoon into the holes of the muffin tins and bake for 15–20 minutes.
4 Leave in the tin for 1 minute, then scoop out and serve warm.

Cook's tip To freeze the muffins, cool them first. To reheat from frozen, thaw first and then reheat in a warm oven at Gas Mark 5/190°C/fan oven 170°C for a few minutes or heat in a microwave for a few seconds.

Make the Most of Your Ingredients

Cheese: hard cheeses
If cheese, such as reduced fat Cheddar or Parmesan, dries out, don't throw it away but keep it well-wrapped in the fridge. Grate and sprinkle 1 tablespoon over grilled fish for the last minute of cooking. Alternatively, stir the same amount into scrambled eggs or sprinkle into simple salads. Grill large Portobello mushrooms and sprinkle with 1 tablespoon of grated half fat cheese for the last few minutes of cooking. Remember to add 1 *ProPoints* value per serving for 1 teaspoon of Parmesan, 2 *ProPoints* values per serving for 1 tablespoon of Parmesan and 3 *ProPoints* values per serving for 40 g (1½ oz) half fat Cheddar.

Cheese: low fat soft cheese
It takes just a little soft cheese to make a tasty snack with tomatoes. Put some halved tomatoes, cut side up, in a foil-lined grill pan. Dot the tomatoes with 25 g (1 oz) low fat soft cheese and plenty of freshly ground black pepper. Grill until golden. The *ProPoints* values per serving will be 1.

Split open an 225 g (8 oz) potato, baked in its skin, dot with 25 g (1 oz) low fat soft cheese and return to the oven for 10–15 minutes until the cheese is melted and bubbling, for 6 *ProPoints* values per serving.

Cheese: reduced fat Greek salad cheese
Crumble 15 g (½ oz) reduced fat Greek salad cheese into hot cooked peas with 1 teaspoon of chopped fresh mint just before serving. Add 1 *ProPoints* value per serving.

Crème fraîche, half fat
Spoon 1 tablespoon of half fat crème fraîche into 60 g (2 oz) hot cooked sweetcorn (2 *ProPoints* values per serving) with a little chopped chilli. Use it to fill a baked 150 g (5½ oz) sweet potato for 7 *ProPoints* values per serving in total.

Eggs
If eggs are getting close to their use by date, you can freeze them for up to 3 months, but first separate them into yolks and whites and freeze them separately. Remember to label how many eggs are in each container. You need to beat the egg yolks with a pinch of salt before freezing.

Fruit
Squeeze oranges which are past their best and freeze the juice in ice cube trays ready to add to salad dressings, soups and sauces (especially tomato-based ones).

If a recipe only uses the zest and juice of ½ a lemon, grate all the zest and squeeze all the juice and freeze the remainder in ice cube trays or keep in a small jar in the fridge for up to 3 days.

Ginger
Keep peeled ginger in the freezer to avoid waste. Grate from frozen.

A little ginger can be grated and mixed into 100 g (3½ oz) 0% fat Greek yogurt then stirred through a mix of chopped apple, pear and orange segments for breakfast.

Ham, Prosciutto
Grill any leftover slices of prosciutto ham for a couple of minutes until crispy, then crumble into soups or salads. 1 slice is 1 *ProPoints* value per serving, 2 thin slices (34 g/1¼ oz) are 2 *ProPoints* values per serving.

Herbs, fresh
Any leftover herbs can be chopped and frozen in sealable bags. Use from frozen in soups and stir-fries.

Mushrooms
Tired mushrooms will still add flavour to stir-fries, so chop them up finely and add with the other vegetables.

Cook finely chopped mushrooms with the onions when making a Bolognese recipe.

Pesto
Leftover pesto freezes well. Spoon it into ice cube trays to use from frozen. 1 tablespoon (15 g/½ oz) is 2 *ProPoints* values per serving.

Spread 1 level teaspoon pesto on a 165 g (5¾ oz) skinless boneless chicken breast before grilling for 5 *ProPoints* values per serving.

Stir 1 level teaspoon of pesto into every two beaten eggs for omelettes or scrambled eggs for 5 *ProPoints* values per serving.

Salsa: tomato ready made salsa
Toss 25 g (1 oz) ready made tomato salsa with 1 hot, reduced fat, thick sausage for 4 *ProPoints* values per serving. Or mix 25 g (1 oz) ready made tomato salsa with the juice of 1 orange and spoon over a 130 g (4½ oz) salmon fillet, grilled, for 6 *ProPoints* values per serving or over a 165 g (5¾ oz) skinless boneless chicken breast, grilled, for 4 *ProPoints* values per serving.

Sunflower seeds
Toast sunflower seeds in a dry frying pan for a few minutes then keep in an airtight container ready to sprinkle into salads. 1 tablespoon (10 g/¼ oz) is 2 *ProPoints* values.

Sweet chilli sauce
A little sauce left in the jar or bottle (about 1–2 teaspoons) can be stirred into 150 g (5½ oz) hot cooked rice or cooked egg noodles to serve as a tasty accompaniment. 2 tablespoons (30 g/1¼ oz) of sweet chilli sauce are 2 *ProPoints* values per serving.

Thai curry pastes
If you like a bit of heat, stir Thai curry paste into a salad dressing. 1 teaspoon (15 g/½ oz) is 1 *ProPoints* value.

Spread 1 teaspoon of Thai curry paste, mixed with a squeeze of lime, over 90 g (3¼ oz) cod fish fillet for 2 *ProPoints* values or 130 g (4½ oz) raw salmon for 6 *ProPoints* values before steaming.

Spice up a simple stir-fry of vegetables with an Eastern flavour by stirring in 1 teaspoon (15 g/½ oz) red Thai curry paste for 1 *ProPoints* value per serving.

ProPoints value Index

Soups & Salads

0 ProPoints values
Beetroot in a bag 19 V

1 ProPoints value
Hot and sour mushroom soup 14 V

2 ProPoints values
Black eyed bean salad 24 V
Summer greens soup 10 V

3 ProPoints values
Moroccan spice pot 16 V
Red lentil salad with Greek dressing 22 V
Spiced cauliflower and cumin soup 12 V

4 ProPoints values
Double bean and ham bowl 10
Ham and pear salad 20
Lemon and artichoke salad 19 V
Parsnip and rosemary soup 12 V

5 ProPoints values
Bonfire soup 9 V
Chicken noodle broth 18
Smoky haddock chowder 14
Spicy pork pho 16

8 ProPoints values
Spiced turkey and couscous salad 22

Meat-free & Sides

0 ProPoints values
Carrot and cumin mash 30 V
Okra Indian style 34 V
Oven-roasted ratatouille 32 V

1 ProPoints value
Honeyed red onion marmalade 28 V
Sweet 'n' sour shallots 32 V

2 ProPoints values
Roasted squash wedges 27 V
Thai slaw 30 V
Vegetable medley with creamy mushrooms 48 V

3 ProPoints values
Moroccan aubergines 53 V
Three veg fritters with poached egg 52 V

4 ProPoints values
Omelette and spinach cannelloni 40 V
Roasted onions with sweet potato 42 V
Stuffed courgettes 48 V
Thai omelette 38 V

5 ProPoints values
Baked pepper eggs 40 V
Chilli lime noodles 34 V
Grilled aubergines with feta dressing 28 V
Spanish stew 46 V

6 ProPoints values
Mediterranean penne pasta 38 V
Pinto and pumpkin casserole 46 V

7 ProPoints values
Fusilli with light spring vegetables 44 V
Mixed bean wrap 42 V
Spiced lentil and egg supper 36 V

8 ProPoints values
Japanese tofu noodles 50 V
Open mushroom lasagne 39 V

9 ProPoints values
Spring greens risotto 36 V
Sweet potato patties with chilli salsa 44 V

11 ProPoints values
Simple lentil dal 52 V

Fish & Seafood

4 ProPoints values
Cheesy cod with olives 62
Crispy fillets with roasted garlic sauce 56
Parmesan fish pastries 55
Thai fish cakes 60

5 ProPoints values
Smoky seafood stew 62

6 ProPoints values
Roasted fish with bean mash 56

8 ProPoints values
Mackerel fillets with fennel slaw 60
Spiced rice and seafood bowl 64

11 ProPoints values
Lemony linguine with trout 58
Pappardelle noodle pot 64

Meat & Poultry

2 ProPoints values
Italian-style chicken livers 72

3 ProPoints values
Mediterranean marrow 78

4 ProPoints values
Stuffed turkey breast 74

5 ProPoints values
American-style beans 78
Chicken in the pot 68
Chicken spring rolls 71
Chicken with a ginger and orange sauce 70
Chicken, squash and spinach filo pie 72
Pork polpette with pepper stew 67
Turkey stew with lentils and spinach 82

7 ProPoints values
Open chicken and vegetable sandwich 70
Zesty pork with spring vegetable stew 74

8 ProPoints values
Beef and vegetable stew 86
Chilli beef ramen 86
Hot beef pockets 90
Mexican salad with cheesy tortillas 80
Turkey and vegetables with quinoa 68

9 ProPoints values
Calzone 84
Saucy Mediterranean stew 80

10 ProPoints values
Baked sweet potatoes with spicy mince and beans 88
Beef and mushroom stroganoff 92
Lamb and chick pea burgers 82
Pork with fennel and rice 76
Steak with black beans and corn salsa 90

Bakes & Puddings

1 ProPoints value
Savoury red pepper muffins 106 V

2 ProPoints values
Baked apples 98 V
Ginger biscuits 100 V
Lemon yogurt ice with hot blueberries 95 V
Savoury rosemary oatcakes 104 V

3 ProPoints values
Courgette tear-and-share loaf 102 V
Hot berry roll ups 98 V
Meringue and ice cream peaches 96 V
Seeded rolls 105 V

4 ProPoints values
Chocolate sponge 100 V
Golden tea loaf 104 V

5 ProPoints values
Orange Bramley crumble 96 V

General Index